DRAMA AND THE WEATHER

Paul Green

DRAMA AND THE WEATHER

Some Notes and Papers on Life and the Theatre

Samuel French, Inc.

25 West 45th Street
New York 36

7623 Sunset Blvd.
Hollywood 46

TORONTO

LONDON

FOR

ELIZABETH

Most of these articles and essays have appeared in magazines, in critical anthologies and as prefaces and printed addresses. Thanks are due to *Theatre Arts*, *The New York Times*, *The Torch*, *The Carolina Quarterly*, Samuel French, Inc., the University of North Carolina Press, and the North Carolina Alpha Chapter of Phi Beta Kappa for the right to republish them here in revised form, and to the University of Oklahoma Press for "Symphonic Drama" from *Ten Talents in the American Theatre*.

Contents

	Page
SYMPHONIC OUTDOOR DRAMA: A SEARCH FOR NEW THEATRE FORMS	1
DRAMA AND THE WEATHER	45
ON THE DEMOCRATIC IDEAL	54
THE ARTIST'S CHALLENGE	61
INTERPRETING AMERICA	69
THE THEATRE AND THE SCREEN	84
MAN AND HIS UNIVERSE	96
FOREVER GROWING: A CREDO FOR TEACHERS	100
LOVE, HATE AND TRAGEDY	114
CHALLENGE TO CITIZENSHIP	118
AGAIN THE SOUTHERN NEGRO	140
ART AND RELIGION	149
FOREWORD TO THE LOST COLONY	153
FREDERICK H. KOCH	162
THE EPIC OF JAMESTOWN	166
VOICE FROM ASIA	177
THE PLAYWRIGHT IN REVOLT	180
A VISIT TO HARDY'S DORCHESTER	185

DRAMA AND THE WEATHER

Symphonic Outdoor Drama: A Search for New Theatre Forms

Back in the winter of 1916, Professor Norman Foerster and I stood in his classroom there in the old Alumni Building in Chapel Hill and talked about the mysterious matter of writing a play—he a young associate professor of English at that time and I a student only a few years younger. After many a plan and hope deferred, I had finally come up from a farm in eastern North Carolina to go to school at the university—come up from years of plowing, cleaning new grounds in the winter, chopping and picking cotton, pitching baseball, and writing shy and useless verses sitting in the woods on many a wide and soundless Sunday afternoon. I had taught country school, too, for two years to save up money enough for a try at college.

The Senior Class had decided to put on an outdoor play at the little hillside theatre just off the campus. A contest had been announced and the prize-winning script would be honored with a production at commencement time. A short play of some thirty or forty minutes in length was needed, Professor Foerster said.

"Why don't you try for it?" he said.

"I wish I could," I answered.

"This is your first year here, but that doesn't matter. It's open to anybody."

"I don't know anything about playwriting," I said. "I don't know how to begin. I've never even seen a play."

"You get yourself some characters and put them to talking, to acting, to doing things."

"Yes, sir, but what sort of characters and what things?"

"That's what you have to decide—that's what your plot, your subject matter will be—what they talk about and what they do. Since this is to be produced by the Senior Class, the contest terms suggest that something to do with the university life here would be preferable. Why don't you read Dr. Battle's history, and perhaps you'll come on some incident or character that would interest you?"

So I got Professor Battle's two-volume history of the university and read its total of seventeen hundred pages, statistics, alumni roll calls and all. It was unbearably dull, as such books perhaps must be, but one of the happenings recounted in it interested me. It had to do with the occupation of Chapel Hill by the Federal soldiers in 1865. A young brigadier general was in charge of these Yankee occupation troops, and to the shame and horror of the bitter and defeated townspeople, he fell in love with the daughter of the university president, and she with him. The courtship of these two young people was a scandal, and the scandal grew greater when the wedding was finally held in the little chapel there under the wide oak and cedar trees. Prayers of vengeance were raised against President Swain, and apparently some of them were heard on high. For shortly after this, the horse he had received as a gift from the young general ran away with him, overturned the buggy, and fatally injured him.

I wrote my play about this love affair, entitled it *A Surrender to the Enemy*, and it won first prize. I have suspected since that it was the only script the committee received. I shall never forget that spring afternoon when it was produced and I sat on the bare hillside among the audience and sweated streams down my face and under my clothes. I felt the eyes of everybody on me. But they weren't. There was enough of talking and moving and mixing of costumes and color down on the popping plank stage to keep them interested—where a garrulous old colored woman was serving as a go-between for the young lovers, and the irate father was fulminating in windy blasts against the North; and where the mother was trying to keep peace and help love on to its normal conclusion; and the young general, with his homemade uniform and shining, scabbarded sword, was keeping up his intent to win his sweet and lovely Southern belle; and she in turn was encouraging him on with a lot of longing, eyelashed looks and expressive workings of her little heirloom fan.

In the end, of course, love won over politics and war, and everybody seemed happy—at least on the stage they did.

II

The European war was now thickening over the Western world and enshrouding the United States. And inspired by the idealism of Woodrow Wilson, I enlisted to go to France and help make the world safe for democracy. And, too, I had already decided to be a poet, and from what I had read and heard I knew that a poet must have experience—experience in hardship, pain, and struggle. And what better place to get them than in a war where there was plenty of bleeding and death?

Then in the long hours of digging ditches and marching and drilling in several army camps in this country, I grew depressed, discouraged, and frustrated. I began reading

philosophy and religion furiously in my spare hours to ease
me—Tolstoy, the New Testament, Buddhism, Nietzsche,
Kant, and Hegel. And I wrote a lot of poetry. It was no
good, but it helped me some. I selected two or three dozen
poems from the hundreds that I had written and had them
published by a local printer in near-by Greenville, South
Carolina. It occurred to me that I might be killed in France,
and this little book would be something of a sign to tell
how I wanted to go in the world.

So finally I sailed away and landed in France, and ultimately in the muddy and death-rotted trenches of Flan-
ders. Sitting deep in the oozy, dripping earth at night, with
the mumble and angry growling of the guns above me, I
kept on writing poetry and sending it out to be mailed to
magazines back home. But so far as I know, not a single
piece of it was ever published, except a short one in *The
Ladies' Home Journal*. I finally realized that raw and actual
experience did not necessarily always help free the imagination into glory. It too often destroyed it. And I thought a
lot about this.

Then as the months went by, and I saw more and more
of the wastage of death and decay, of the red tooth and
claw of survival, the perishing away of all the finer instincts and purposes of the men and boys about me, as
they tried to kill and keep from being killed, I realized
that peace would never come through violence, love would
never come through hate, and brotherhood of brother
could not survive the killing of the other brother. At least
I thought so. And I determined that some day and in some
way I would write about these things. Maybe I could not
do it in poetry, but perhaps in stories, in novels, or in plays
even.

And all the while I was saving what money I could. And
when I moved up from private to sergeant and then at last

to second lieutenant, I saved more. And with the war ended, I had enough to go back to the University of North Carolina.

Meanwhile I had grown more and more interested in religion and philosophy. Only in these could I find some sort of answer to the troubles that tortured me—the meaning of my life and what I was here for, and what others like me were here for. And back at the university I won a sixty-dollar philosophy prize, and that encouraged me in that subject. About this time Professor Edwin Greenlaw, head of the English department at the university, brought Frederick H. Koch in from North Dakota to teach playwriting and tap the rich stores of North Carolina folklore, legend, and song. And Koch was the man needed. He believed that everybody was a playwright more or less, and the amazing thing was that he got the folks around him to believe it. And a great stew of playmaking soon got started.

I joined the playwriting class somewhat on the side and began turning out one-act plays along with Tom Wolfe, Wilbur Stout, Hubert Heffner, Elizabeth Lay, George Denny, John Terry, Harold Williamson, and many others. My main purpose still was philosophy, and I looked forward to getting my doctorate and teaching in that field. But at odd hours I wrote a lot of plays, and a number of them were produced at Chapel Hill. Then I won a fifteen-hundred-dollar fellowship in philosophy, and that determined me. Elizabeth Lay and I got married, and we set off to Cornell, where I was to do graduate work.

But I couldn't quit writing plays. And during my stay at that university I wrote dozens of them, all short ones. It was great fun. And many a night I hammered my typewriter through the long hours and joyfully saw the sun come up—writing about the Negroes and the poor whites of my boyhood remembering in eastern North Carolina, and pouring out on page after page my indignation at their piteous and doleful lot. Then a call came for me to return to Chapel Hill to teach philosophy. And there I kept at teaching for many years. But all the while I had a type-writer in my office, and between classes and conferences with students I would get in short spasms of work. I sent a couple of short Negro folk plays off to *Poet-lore*, and they were published. Then I sent one to *Theatre Arts Monthly*. Mrs. Isaacs, the editor, wrote me an encouraging letter and published it. Then the next year the Dallas Little Theatre of Texas entered this play, *The No 'Count Boy*, in the contest for the Belasco Cup in New York. The group won the cup, and a few days later I had a wire from Henry Holt offering me a contract for a book of one-act pieces, with a sizable financial advance. And the birds sang to me from every bush on the campus as I walked home in the evening. I had had a play done on Broadway. True, a short play but still done on Broadway.

Holt published my book, *The Lord's Will and Other Plays*, and then Robert McBride brought out six short Negro plays; and the next year, 1928, Samuel French pub-lished another volume, *In the Valley and Other Carolina Folk Plays*. Meanwhile I was working on longer things. In 1926, I sent two full-length plays up to New York, and they were both produced in that season, one of them, *In Abraham's Bosom* winning the Pulitzer Price. I attended some of the rehearsals of the other, *The Field God*, and made my first acquaintance with the professional New York theatre. I saw a number of Broadway shows, too, and with the exception of O'Neill's *The Emperor Jones* and the wonderful Jewish folk drama *The Dybbuk*, I was disap-pointed in what I saw. Maybe these two dramas should have satisfied me for all the sorry ones. But they didn't.

Perhaps I was expecting too much from Broadway. I met a lot of theatre people and shared in a number of high-cackling cocktail parties, and I grew more and more unhappy. I had to do these things mostly at weekends and at holidays, for I was carrying on my full-time work in philosophy at the university.

I learned about the star system, unions, and contracts, and rents, and guilds, and agents' commissions. These I realized were necessary, but the lack seemed to me to be in the dramas themselves. Something I wanted wasn't there. In my frustration, I struck out with some experiments and wrote a few bitter plays, among them *Tread the Green Grass* and *Shroud My Body Down*. They were sick, wild things and pretty formless. *Tread the Green Grass* went into rehearsal at the Greenwich Village Theatre under the direction of Jimmy Light, but it was too much for even that hardened theatre man and was given up a week or so before it was to open.

Pretty soon I was tired of the Broadway theatre. Even my own plays tired me, and after the final dress rehearsals, I couldn't sit through them again. I had never had this trouble with certain motion pictures that I liked, for example *The Birth of a Nation* and the German picture *Variety*. And certainly never could I get enough of Charlie Chaplin's work. I saw *The Gold Rush* fourteen times. There was something missing in the so-called legitimate drama—missing for me and missing in me.

I had read a lot of Shakespeare by now, of course, and could not dare hope to find any comparable richness of imagery and beauty in the language of any of the Broadway and modern plays. I didn't expect that. I also had read a lot of the Greek dramas and books on them, and I had imagined their wonderful productions and thought that I would have liked them had I been alive in those days—and I knew that

I would like them now if they could be reproduced with the chanting, the flute and the harp, the choreography, and the imaginative movements of the actors in those ancient times. I went to musical comedies, and they seemed empty and worthless, too. Gradually I began to realize that the Broadway theatre was the theatre of mass entertainment and was meant to indulge the passing crowd and to make money. No doubt, as I say, in my ignorance and high-mindedness I had come expecting too much. I banged off a piece about it all as an introduction to a theatre anthology in which I said, with youthful fervency:

"I found, it seemed to me, that the American professional stage—and that is to say the New York stage—is an industry and not an art as I had dreamed; that it is a business run to the pattern of supply and demand, with its standards of excellence derived from the general wants of the buyers. Such a method may not be so bad as it concerns matters of sentiment, slapstick, and farcical vaudeville, for these take their rise from and prosper in a milieu of mediocrity and standardized emotions. They make no absurd claims. They are the theatre of entertainment, and in their honesty we can enjoy them. But this is not enough. The serious theatre —the higher professional drama—appears to be neither the one nor the other. I went to it again and again. I went behind the scenes, I talked with stagehands and saw the workings of the unions, heard the complaints of tired actors, arguments and interpretations from the directors and impresarios, saw fights and quarrelings of peevish stars as to the size of their names in electric lights, jealousies and backbitings, listened to the 'how will that go?' the 'what will she gross?' and 'they won't stand for that;' saw publicity and its methods, read facts and figures on salaries, rents, contracts, censorship and equity, investments, overhead, receipts, the box-office—and all these spoke of dog eat dog and look to your suspenders."

III

A New York theatre friend of mine, Barrett Clark, who spent much time traveling out into the land lecturing on the American drama, told me that I need never expect to find my kind of high-minded theatre on Broadway. "What you are looking for," he said, "is what might be called the 'New Theatre,' the theatre of the imagination—is that right?"

"Yes, I guess that's right," I said.

"Well then, there is such a theatre—not out in the provinces, not in the schools and universities and civic centers—no—but right here in New York."

"Where in New York?"

"Among the independent groups," he said, "and there are many of them."

"Well, if there are such groups—like the old perished Provincetown—funny I haven't heard of them."

"Most of them are small, obscure, but they are trying. Go and see."

So I did—hunting for the theatre of splendid creation, of imagination and the dream. And I got acquainted with what might be called the "arty theatres." I found them living in squalor and misery in the dark places of the great city. And there I found the symbol for the thing, the pose for the content, attitudinizing and gesturing, and talk, talk, talk—talk of a vorticist and cubistic kind, and always with plenty of social philosophizing about the weird and decadent state of the world, including our own America—talk about how Freud had been born to set man free in his insides. These devotees were the sleepless, unbathed, and disheveled ones, young people who mostly had come from all parts of the country into the bright metropolis to find expression for their souls, the space to stretch their wider-reaching arms, not finding room enough in the thousand-mile prairies or in the big, broad fields of the South. And here they had spun downward into this quagmire of confusion and frustration.

But they were brave and determined, these young people, and they comforted one another in the certainty of their pure devotion to the ideal of art. And I listened to their proud aesthetic, which they had developed mainly from hearsay and secondhand out of Europe, out of Russia, and with a mixture of our own American creed of psychological behaviorism thrown in. They pooh-poohed the idea of money. And there were long and dawn-breaking after-performance discussions in some cheerless apartment about soul and spiritual form, about inner releases and outward expressions, about the curves of desire and turgid glots and spouts of significance, and about ecstacy and the great unconscious. And there was much quoting from Isadora Duncan, Gordon Craig, and from Freud again, and the then-popular John B. Watson.

And on their little stages that I visited I found an ever increasing din of carpentry and constructivism, of strange contraptions to make clear the dramatic meaning sought. I remember one little run-down studio where I was shown the setup for a piece entitled *Man Is Man*, with credit for the idea to Gertrude Stein. And sticking up in front of the color-smeared, outlandish backdrop was a huge hand, tall as my head.

"That's the hand of God you see there," said the enthusiastic and grimy young director. "It stays there through every scene."

"But doesn't the constant sight of the hand distract from the action of the play itself? I believe I'd be looking at the hand all the time."

"That's what we want you to do."

"But shouldn't I watch the actors?"

"You'll watch them both—for the meaning of the action is emphasized as it were, made significantly symbolic by the hand itself."

"I'd rather see the hand in my imagination, let it be referred to in the script maybe, and—"

"No, no. You are wrong. You should just go read the last issue of *The Mask* magazine."

"I read it, and I remember it says," I answered a little coldly, "that Shakespeare was not a good playwright—said he was too long-winded, diffuse, poetical, and the like."

"Yes, and I think he is."

"Then what about Goethe, Hebbel, the earlier and later Ibsen? What about Racine, and what about Ansky who wrote *The Dybbuk?* And what about J. M. Synge and his *Playboy of the Western World*, William Butler Yeats and *Cathleen ni Houlihan*, and Paul Claudel with his *Tidings Brought to Mary?*"

"I don't know all of them, but if *The Mask* says they're not good theatre, then I agree."

"But their works are representative of the 'New Theatre' you talk about," I went on, and a little sharply now, "the theatre of the imagination. They don't find it necessary to provide all this carpentry work. They use language to suggest, to connote, to lead the imagination, as it were, through the walls of the theatre out into spaces of freedom and beyond. Their theatre is for me *the* theatre of the imagination—using for the dress and facts of environment just enough of actuality to suggest and help the imagination in the course of its flight. It seems you would kill the imagination. Take Shakespeare. His greatness lies in the very words you seek to delete. Don't novels, poems, and great plays of the past—the Book of Job, The Ancient Mariner—don't they prove the superiority of the mind over the factualities of the eye and the ear?"

"Now you're talking about books, about literature. Well, I tell you the theatre is not a literary art."

"That's the very point. You try to make it a literary art by trying to force it to take the place of literature. And I should think that to be the great falsity of the new theatre's measure and use of such strangely contrary souls as the constructivist Meyerhold, the lurid and visionary Strindberg, Freud with his sex dreams, and the allegorical William Blake—these the patron saints of the new theatre. This is false mysticism, it seems to me, if ever there was such. What I find here is much like a scene in the movie version of *Pilgrim's Progress*, where Christian's soul is taken up to heaven. And this soul was shown as an object about two feet long. And that is really your watchword and election sure, isn't it?—everything an object—whether the need is for mood and impression, a splendor of shining poetry, or digging dialogue of ideas—like God's hand there? Well, this soul was packaged, wrapped in white, and was carried up the mountainside by some dozen women dressed supposedly like angels. How dull and factual it all was! Let the children, let the grownups read the book. Let their minds fill and throb and reach to all the simple but rich poetry of old Bunyan himself—with his description of the higher clouds and the pilgrims sweetly talking of the celestial city where the heavenly shining ones, riding on the wings of the wind, met their mighty Lord of Glory with trumpets and songs of praise. The dramatists of the *Oresteia, Faust, Lear,* and *A Midsummer Night's Dream* knew enough. They have shown us the way. No, the truth is, lacking the power of words, we've taken refuge in mechanics, haven't we?"

"Then I can see you won't want any tickets for our play," said the young director with a weary, pitying smile.

"I'm afraid not," I said. "I've only seen the hand of the play, and when I think of the God who scooped out the seas, piled up the mountains, and with His finger marked the course of great rivers down in my country, the God who hurls thunderbolts and rends the heavens asunder with sheets of water and flame, who turns the planets in their courses and stirs the whirling nebulae in eternal time and infinite space—when I consider this, then this constructed hand becomes puny, dead, lifeless and cheap."

"All right, all right," he burst out.

I had a charge on, and I went off and wrote my feelings down in my notebook, saying: "And so I came back from there—back where the elements of the new theatre I believed in—the theatre of the imagination—were to be experienced scattered and apart, for there they long had been—back to the true make-believe of the marionettes, up to the cathedral with its mystic chant and ritual pantomime, back to the art gallery, or the circus, or concert, or athletic field, or to my room with a copy of Apuleius, Aeschylus, or Sophocles, or Haigh's *Attic Theatre*, or to the university library for another book wherein to re-vision Beelzebub squatted on a wave in hell and the drunken crew of Greece raging in the woods, or to the movies where Emil Jannings wakes in his sour bed the morning after and Charlie Chaplin walks so exquisitely between two worlds. For in all these, now existing somewhat apart—marionettes, painting, sculpture, and architecture, the dance, music, folk song, and ballad, legend, music, religious ritual, and the dance, circus and stadium spectacle, the written and spoken word, the sleeper's dream, the movies, the world of work and machinery even—in all these are to be found those elements which could be drawn on, elements which some-day will receive their proper fusion in the new theatre, the theatre of imagination, of lofty common sense."

And I began to work on another play for Broadway, in which I hoped to use some of those elements.

IV

About this time Barrett Clark suggested that I try for a Guggenheim Fellowship to go to Europe and have a look at the theatre there. "You'll learn a lot there," he said. And so when the prized award came through, I got a leave of absence from philosophy teaching at Carolina and with my wife and two children set out. I landed in Berlin, where the best theatre in the world was supposed to be at that time. I saw a lot of shows and opera. And true, I learned a lot. And I kept filling my notebooks with comments all the time.

I went to many plays at different theatres—at the Schau-spielhaus, the Schiller, the Lessing, the Berliner, the Deutsches, the Volksbühne, the Metropol, the Renaissance, and others. Three opera houses were running, and I saw much opera, too. And there were playwrights everywhere— 192 practicing professional ones in Germany at that time— according to a literary yearbook I read. And actors, singers, designers, and technicians were everywhere too. The plays ranged from Tolstoy's *The Living Corpse* to *Abie's Irish Rose,* and there was much emphasis on homosexual and neurotic themes in between. For all its activity, I found the German theatre a pretty sick one. The frustration and defeat of World War I were heavy on the people, and inflation was running wild. The future looked harsh and drear, and the name of Adolf Hitler, the man with hope in his raging voice, was beginning to be heard. Perhaps it was no wonder that a subjective expressionism and a personal idiom of self-analysis were so evident in the drama being produced.

"Maybe you just don't like the theatre," my wife said to me one night as we returned home over the crunched snow. We had just been to see a depressing piece about sex aberrations among German youth. "Maybe you ought to go back home and write stories and novels."

"Maybe I ought," I said.

"You rather liked the *Dreigroschenoper* by Weill and Brecht."

"Yes. The people were a sorry lot, but there was something about the way the music and the story mixed together that I liked."

"Why don't you try to get more music in your plays, more dance?"

"Yes, I always like good music in plays, especially folk music and dancing too, some kind of dancing. They can be very beautiful—like the weird beggars' dance in *The Dybbuk*. But I seem to be bad as anybody else when I sit down to write my folk pieces—it's always ugliness and violence, and somebody killing somebody, and this person or that going crazy. Words seem to come easier when I write about terrible and pathetic things. I don't understand it."

"You've written some good comic things, too, *The No 'Count Boy, Quare Medicine*, and—and—" she spoke up loyally.

One night I was invited to a party given by a German newspaper editor to honor the American millionaire and art-sponsor Otto Kahn. I had met Mr. Kahn back in New York the year before. He had asked me to have lunch with him down in his palatial Wall Street office. And there while he ate his milk and mush, and I ham and eggs, he had talked encouragingly to me about the theatre. He was a fine, sympathetic man and was always ready to help beginners in the arts, whatever the field. "Get out of North Carolina," he said, "get out and broaden yourself. Find new subject matter to write about. Folk things are all right, maybe, to begin with. But they're too narrow, too provincial. If you're going to be a real playwright, you must write about things that count."

We renewed our acquaintance at the party, and he said he was glad that I had taken his advice and got out to see what was being done in Europe.

"But I'm still writing folk plays," I said.

"In time, in time," he answered with a smile. "There's another folk theatre man here," he went on, "just come from Russia with his Yiddish repertory troupe—Alexis Granowsky."

"I've been reading about him in the papers," I answered eagerly. "I'd like to meet him."

He took me over and introduced me, and Granowsky and I had a good talk. From the first I was keenly interested in his ideas. "In my theatre there are three things I emphasize—music, pantomime, and the word," he said.

"You put music first then?" I queried.

"Perhaps I do. I hope you'll come and see some of our plays. We are opening next week at the Theater des Westens on Kantstrasse."

I went and was delighted. I went again and again, and I decided that if I had seen nothing else in Europe, this Moscow Jewish Academy Theatre would have been worth my coming. True, here again was much of the symbolism and constructivism of the confused new theatre followers back home. But there was more. Except for that impassioned and wonderful story of religious ecstacy and human love, *The Dybbuk*, I had never seen any modern plays that were more lyrical and intense in their productions. Such use of music, pantomime, acrobatics, masks even, and energized properties! And such rhythmic harmony of ensemble acting! It seemed as if the director had deliberately meant to fuse all the elements of theatre art into one. And later I learned that that was just what he was attempting. One of the plays I saw, *A Night in the Old Marketplace,* was a sort of grotesque, tragic carnival, with hardly any dialogue or spoken words, nearly all pantomime, dance, and musicalized action. It, too, dealt with decay and death, but with such verve and even comic satire that a sense of liveliness and zest spilled over from the footlights. The old market in the center of a small Jewish town was made a sort of symbol of a failing and degenerate world. The characters in the play—members of the synagogue, visitors to the brothel, all kinds and types—were confused and frustrated enough, but hanging tenaciously on to life. Finally the dead were raised out of their graves, and the living found to their astonishment that there was no difference between these dead and themselves. As part of the new Russian creed, the play seemed to declare that the old world and its times were perished, and those who believed in them were as good as perished, too. Distorted masks, a ghastly stage setting, queer, outlandish dances added to the gripping effect of the play.

And then there was an eccentric piece, *The Travels of Benjamin III.* Granowsky had taken an old Jewish folk tale and adapted it in his free theatre manner. He showed two Jewish friends who set out adventuring through the world in search of some of the ancient glory of their Jewish heritage. Actually, the play was a sort of dream in which all kinds of miraculous things happened. One of the Jews married the daughter of the Mogul of India and adopted the title of Benjamin III, King of the Jews. Later, the two comrades came to their senses and returned home to their little village, better and wiser men. They now realized and declared that the reality of life was to be found in their everyday village work and living, and not in fancies and dream escapism.

There was no hang-over of ancient Jewish pessimism or sorrow in these plays. The actors were buoyant, strong, and vital even in scenes of despair. Here was the will to live, to create, to be strong and build, build for the future, to build the Russian socialist republic. Apart from all politics, I felt the power and freshness of Granowsky's theatre. And I was eager to talk with him again.

He received me in his apartment, glum and downcast for some reason. But my high praise and enthusiasm for his plays evidently cheered him up a bit.

"I am glad you liked us," he said. "What pleased you most about our productions?"

"I don't know. I liked it all—the acting, the dances, and, I guess, especially the music."

"Ah, the music," he spoke up eagerly, "that is it. Mine is first a musical theatre, last a musical theatre."

"But not musical comedy."

"Oh no, not that, not musical comedy as in America. Our plays are real, full of life; they say something."

"A social message."

"Yes, but always in terms of the theatre, I am more interested in the theatre than politics."

"I wish you could bring your group to America. It would mean a lot to us. We need to see the sort of thing you are doing."

"Ah, America. I want to go there. Mr. Otto Kahn has offered to guarantee us a few weeks in New York. I have appealed to Moscow for permission. I am waiting."

"Wonderful. And then you think you will go?"

"There is much strong feeling between the two countries. Still, I have asked permission. And I may tell you that I may not be wise in asking this permission."

"Why not?"

"These politics—I am awaiting the answer, as I told you." And he smiled a little wan smile, his gaze indrawn as if some inner apprehension or dolefulness bothered him. Then he shook his head and went on. "I am glad you liked our —music drama."

"I remember Wagner's 'music dramas.'"

"But they were operas. Music swallowed up the words, submerged them, changed their real and actual meaning. I use music—and the same for dance, pantomime, costume, properties, and setting—to interpret the words, to give them a richer meaning. I have been working in this type of drama now for ten years, and every day convinces me that I have just begun to glimpse the possibilities. Here is the truly free theatre—I mean it is ahead. For instance, musicalized pantomime, speech, facial expressions, and bodily movements can liberate all those imaginative human meanings which straight realism or even the most poetic language itself can never completely do. Yes, music is the word. With music and stylization of the proper sort, one can obtain short cuts in scenery, properties, and in moving the story forward. It is easier to get right down to business, go right to the heart of your dramatic matter, to reach the inner meaning and symbolism even of the story you have to tell, to make it immediately available to the audience— with music. If I should ever be forced to leave Russia," and once more that wan smile and indrawn, empty look were in his face for an instant, "America is the place I'd want to go to begin my theatre over again. Your nation has everything to make a great theatre movement possible. You are the richest of all countries in dramatic material. You are a country of conflicts. And I don't mean those that result in physical violence necessarily. I mean spiritual conflicts, conflicts of ideas, of individual feelings, of points of view, of mass groupings, of types, of individuals, and of organizations. And always energy, energy. Your country is boundless in that. And think of your many nationalities with their own inheritances of speech and custom. Surely at this hour yours is the most creative nation on the globe. I know something about your theatrical history—I have heard of a few of your pioneer workers—William Vaughn Moody, Percy MacKaye, and, of recent years, Eugene O'Neill. And then there was another man—he wrote some one-act Negro plays."

"Ridgely Torrence."

"Yes, Torrence, that's right. Who else have you?"

"Maxwell Anderson is writing poetic drama now. You may remember his and Laurence Stallings' great success, *What Price Glory?*"

"Yes."

"Some of us are hoping Anderson is beating down a path which will lead toward a new expression of American genius. And there are Sidney Howard, Robert Sherwood, Philip Barry, Marc Connelly, George Kelly, Elmer Rice, Lynn Riggs. . . ."

"Do any of them make a great use of music?"

"Not much. But Connelly in his play *The Green Pastures*, created from a series of religious folk tales by a southern writer, Roark Bradford, used a lot of Negro spirituals."

"Do you use music in your plays?"

"I try to now and then—folk things. And I plan to use a lot of music in the future."

"I hope you will," and he nodded his head encouragingly. "I can't understand why America hasn't developed music drama,"—throwing out his hands nervously. "Well, that is one of these mysteries of art. The impulse and the creation come when they will come. But I prophesy before the real genius of your country can be expressed, can find its statement on the stage, music vitally integrated into the drama itself must be used. For instance, why hasn't America ever created a great Negro theatre? More than once in recent days and under the present regime in my homeland of Russia, I have seriously considered migrating to America to try to build a Negro musical drama there. Think of the singing, the religious rituals and practices, the superstitions, the vivid folk speech, folklore, and tall tales, the dramatic conditions surrounding that submerged yet marvelously gifted people."

"Some beginnings are being made," I said. "When I spoke of Marc Connelly's and Roark Bradford's *Green Pastures*, I should have mentioned DuBose and Dorothy Heyward's Negro folkplay *Porgy*, which uses a lot of music. And then there are Negro drama groups in Harlem, New York; Cleveland, Ohio, in Chicago, and in some of the larger cities. But they are only beginnings."

"I have talked to Mr. Kahn about this too, about such an idea as a Negro theatre in America. And he said he would consider subsidizing it if I would come and organize it. Well, it is a thing to think about, and there is much, much to be done, and let us hope we shall have time and a chance to do it."

I saw Alexis Granowsky once or twice more. I was present at a meeting with him and a few others on the tragic night he reported that his theatre had been dissolved by a command of the Soviet authorities, and his actors had been ordered back to Moscow. This was perhaps the answer he got for his request to take his troupe to America.

He did not return to Russia. Maybe he didn't dare. He moved to Paris, and not long after I heard that he had died there. I never knew why he did not come to America in accordance with this dream he had, instead of going to France.

I stayed on in Berlin through the spring and then moved to England for several months, with a short excursion into France to visit some of the old Paris scenes that I had known during and after the war. The theatre in those two countries was much the same as it had been for generations, and I saw nothing that got hold of me, except parts of Sean O'Casey's *The Silver Tassie* and an English production of Strindberg's cruel and bitter tragedy, *The Father*.

Of course, there was Bernard Shaw. I had a chance to spend an evening with that remarkable man, and we—rather he—talked theatre for hours. "Speech is the thing," he said, "not music, masks, pantomime, or dance. Speech is glorious." He repeated it more than once. "That's all you need in the theatre—a voice with something to say, with ideas that have meaning. All the rest is furbelows and fancies. Words, words, fine and powerful words saying something people need to hear. And if they need it, they'll like it—provided, of course, the playwright knows how to say it interestingly. Shakespeare depended on words, and he did rather well as a playwright now and then in using them. Don't you think so?"

v

When I got back home, I took time off to work with the newly formed Group Theatre in putting on a play that I had written sometime before, *The House of Connelly*, a drama of the old and the new South. It had some critical success and a fairly decent run at the Martin Beck Theatre but made no money. By this time, my family was in need of something more substantial than dramatic theories. So I got a leave of absence from the university and set out for Hollywood. I worked there for many months and ran into plenty of grief as well as money, but that story lies outside this narrative.

When I got back to Chapel Hill, and with my bills paid, I started planning another play for Broadway. (I have written about this play elsewhere but will restate here at some length what I said.)

During my student days at the university, I had often walked out in the evening to the northwestern part of Chapel Hill where the Negroes lived. For generations they had lived here, camped, as it were, under the very eaves of the great gray and red brick buildings of the campus and with little intellectual or spiritual profit from the nearness, so far as I could tell. In and around their poor houses they gathered in the evening, sang their songs, cracked their jokes, carried on their lovemaking, and now and then fell into fights and killings. And each morning they rose to work for the white man—some as cooks and washerwomen, others as janitors at the university, others as bricklayers, yard boys, and waiters in the boardinghouses. I decided to try to write a play about this Negro settlement, with its teeming, upboiling life, its intense emotions, superstitions, frustrations, hopes, and accomplishments, its grievings and dark humilities. I would write not about a single protagonist and antagonist, but about the whole village.

What about a gathering place for my characters? A church would not do, for only the religious life of the people would come to the fore there. I needed a place in which all facets and turns of their habits and actions could be displayed. A boardinghouse seemed the best place then. And as for room to give these people purpose and place to move in, I conceived that a sort of street roadway ran in front of the house, and before the house was a yard. Then as for the house itself, I needed different rooms and levels for the spilling of the action. So I put a porch on the front of the house, where some of the characters now and then could gather and say their say. Then behind the porch, a step higher, the eating room interior, and still another step higher at the back, a lean-to bedroom. Thus, I had four levels of action—the street and yard, the porch, the eating room, and the lean-to. Then at the left of the eating room I joined on a shed bedroom, and out in the yard at the left a little brick barbershop shack, where action, going and coming and moseying about could take place. At the right of the boardinghouse was another narrow street down which people could come now and then. And behind the house I imagined a rising bluff along which a distant and high-balling train could pass, with its shrilling whistle and sparks and smoke, and the Negroes giving their wild, long-ing cry of "Hot damn, hot damn, there she goes!" In and around this boardinghouse with its playing areas I collected my characters—some seventy-five or one hundred of them, all representatives of a cross section of Negro life in the South—a voodoo worker, a preacher, a granny woman, several convicts, a harlot, a beautician, a feeble-minded lad, several day laborers, a singing blind beggar, a sport, cooks, an undertaker, a folk philosopher, a salesman of death in-surance, a barber—and men, women, and children. These last were in the main atmosphere and chorus figures.

What about the time? I must choose a day and hour in which it would be natural for this sprawl of Negro life to come together in such a setting. A Saturday night or after-noon would do. And it must not be in winter, for then my numerous characters wouldn't have the free play of the out-doors to move around and sit about in, and my different acting areas would have no meaning. So it would have to be in summer—and rightly a warm summer evening or night when the hard work of the week had ended, and Sunday with its anthems and sermons and sinners' warnings had not come, and the blue workday Monday was still another day away. At such a sweaty, oozing, and dewy eveningtime, then, the story germ would sprout naturally and grow its pushing way along to the final bloom of explosive fulfillment—after which the Negroes' normal life would return to its deep tide of existence, rest, and the play be over.

As I worked at this drama, I felt myself sitting in a high chair or on a high stump in the middle of the road in front of the house, watching the events take place, seeing the characters coming in here and there as the story required, saying their say, doing their do, and retiring as their inclination and need pulled them off. And I was sitting there with a notebook in my hand writing it all down. And of course there was a sense of will-at-work on my part too, a creative energizing into being all that was happening before my eyes. There was this double dialectic all the while then —the happenings of things and people of themselves and at the same time their being caused to happen consciously and purposely on my part, each character separate and individual as to personality, appearance, dress, behavior, and speech,—among them old Quiviene Lockley, the boarding-house keeper; Willie Lockley, her youngish and feeble-minded husband; Bantam Wilson, a convict broke loose from the roads; Ed Uzzell, the philosopher, with his inner-moan of "Under the tight pot I hear you calling, and oh, seas—rivers of brick and mortar and iron—open the way— let it flow on;" Bad Eye Smith, the drayman, dreaming of money and a new truck to come; Doodle Wilson, the boy preacher, with his song of "Death, oh Death, spare me over another day;" Murdock, the bad man, seeking regeneration and a new name through love and steady work; the black stranger John Henry, the mighty steel-driving man, croaking up from the deep caverns of his breast the awesome statement, "I done sold my soul to the devil and my heart it's turned into stone;" and many, many others.

And often I would leave my chair or stump and find myself up on the porch or in the bedroom right among my characters, close enough to hear them breathing, see the deeps of their eyes and smell the odor of their bodies. In controlling and handling these many characters as they played out their story, I felt that I was in something of the same position as a composer driving forward his composition for some eighty or one hundred instruments, or even as the conductor directing the orchestra which played that composition after it was written. The entire body of the piece must be kept moving itself along, by means of the individual instrumentations that came forward to personal fulfillment, turned, retired, and gave place to others, and they in succession likewise. Character and story motifs must be developed, thematic statements made and exploited, and an upboiling and stewing of symphonic creativity kept going toward a dynamic finale.

And a stern control over the material must be kept all the while. And that control lay in the story line. Whatever failed to advance the story must be left out. For, after all, drama—whether it deals with five people or one hundred— is story-telling through speech and action. Of course, some splurge of language and lyrical aria display could be indulged in, but only for heightened effect. And the fixed idea, as in a Beethoven or Berlioz symphony, the sensed and felt and consciously shaped inner natural form, call it the plot or even melodic line, whether submerged or coming boldly now and then to the surface—as it always must—this fixed idea and intent must control matters.

I kept searching for a term of definition and interpretation to describe my play and to help in its unification as I worked along.

In trying to express the inner lives and their meanings in my Negro community, I found that I was having to call upon about every element available in modern theatrical art. Folk song and poetry were needed, also dance, pantomime, sound effects and chorus voices—and dreams and visions, too, and the grisly microphone for the voice of the white man's law or fearsome God speaking from the sky to his people. Moments of horrification would require masks, and always there must be the liquefication of light to accompany the human behavior at work—light that would illuminate an ever-advancing story point. And in that illumination the mind of the spectator could read the message clear. The fabled fire in the Scriptures was like this light, the furnace fire in which the Hebrew children once stood all bright and glorified. So it seemed to me.

And always there was music—music!

"Music drama" didn't seem the right term for the play. For there was more than music. "Ballad opera" it could not be, nor "opera." "Festival drama" was too loose and "misnoming." "Lyric drama" lacked entirely. Finally, "symphonic drama" seemed right. Yes, a "sounding-together" in the true meaning of the Greek word. And so I adopted the form and have used it for a number of other like dramas that I have written since.

I found in writing this Negro drama that by the symphonic use of the various elements of the theatre, especially music, there came a freedom and fullness of possible story and character statement not otherwise to be had in dealing with large groups of people in action. As Granowsky had said, I found that with the use of music, short cuts and intensifications could be quickly indulged in, which the audience would accept without questioning. Conventions could be quickly established or other conventions dispensed with, and the story beginning, say, could be hatched out of an obstructive matrix without much ado.

And in this kind of theatre, time could be telescoped through a symbol, even could become that symbol, and space could be compressed like the breathing of some huge and delicate accordion of the mind. Tomorrow is already here. A voice of the inner chorus commentator out of my Negro village could say so. And in the thickened moody and musically charged environment, in the climate of credibility established, the audience would agree.

There was a nemesis in this Negro play. A huge and oncoming highway was being built across the earth by the white man and was aimed straight at the Negro settlement. The deep reverberations of dynamite exploding in the hills, clearing the way for this road, sounded ominously and constantly nearer as the drama proceeded.

Passions and hates and loves and fears and whorings were fecundating in this village. During the play murder was committed in the boardinghouse. Then came the wham-wham of a policeman's stick, and the hoarse great voice of the Law was heard bellowing like Behemoth through the valley. Culprits and innocent ones ran this way and that in fear. The Golem tread of justice and retribution came nearer. The reverberations on the distant road sounded closer, louder. Nature herself became sick, upset, violent. A fierce wind whoomed and whistled among the shacks in the valley and around our particular boardinghouse. The limbs of the shade tree in the yard twisted and swung like a gesticulating maniac. A final and terrific explosion occurred in the street at the right. A pandemonium of shrieking and lamentations of the people rose in the valley. The moon dropped down the sky like a shot. And then, with the echoes falling away, the tumult and the terror died. The scene faded gently and musically out. From the darkness came a low and fervent chanted prayer of the persecuted and disordered people. A few heartbeats of time and no more, and the light swam up again.

The iron-snouted, machine-age road had arrived. The nemesis was there. It had plowed its revengeful way through the settlement like a cruel steel colter through an anthill. The old boardinghouse had been pushed aside, the entrails of furniture and pieces of bedding spilled out along the earth. Because of the depravity, the sinfulness, the causeless misery of these sorrowful ones, the road had taken its toll.

A dozen or more of our characters, striped convicts now, were working, digging away on this road, slinging their picks and bringing them down, and ever bring them down in the white blazing sun. The heat of August shimmered across the land. "Lazy Lawrence" danced his fiendish monkey dance in the sun. The sweat poured down, the only cooling dampness in the world for the mourners on that road. On a stump to the left a guard squatted, drowsy, vapid, like a toad. The rifle in the crook of his arm kept alert, its muzzle warned like an eye, it threatened. The convicts dug on and on, their faces set down the infinite stretch of cruel road that reached from the rising to the setting sun. And as their picks came down against the earth with a thud, a husky, desperate, groaning chant burst from their baked lips, carrying on and carrying on over the long deadening hours of pain.

> They call their Jesus—hanh—
> They say their Jesus—hanh—
> They mean their Jesus—hanh—
> Eigh Lord!

In this form of symphonic drama the convicts and the digging had become the road.

The form seemed right then for the expression of such group life, of setting forth the relationships of individuals and their fellows, of masses and crowds affected, energized and motivated as they would be by some centripetal idea and dramatic intent—some story of tradition, of history, of folk inheritance and legend, some famous native character or group of characters splurging themselves forth out of their heritage.

Under the title of *Roll, Sweet Chariot*, the drama opened at the Cort Theatre in New York in the autumn of 1934. A brave-hearted woman, Margaret Hewes, was the producer and Emjo Basshe and Stanley Pratt the directors. It was a sad occasion for all of us. The audience was confused with our experiments. I had insisted that the play run without intermission. And in the pit we had a Negro chorus of twenty-two voices, flanked by timpani and a clarinet, which expressed the joy and grief of the drama in notated wordless vocables. Dolfe Martin had written what I thought and still think was a beautiful score for the chorus. At a crucial moment a fuse blew out in a loud-speaker in the loft with a banshee wail, and our Law and our God became comic. The audience was embarrassed and then rarely tickled.

Out in the lobby I paced up and down during the performance. About midway, Robert Benchley came bursting out of the auditorium and several others with him.

"Intermission or not," he said to me angrily, "I'm going to smoke. What's it all about, anyhow?"

The play closed at the end of the first week and to a half-empty house. The reviews were violently mixed, although a day later I got a wire from the *New York Times* critic commending me for my use of language, and the valiant Edith Isaacs, editor of *Theatre Arts Monthly*, wrote strongly in the play's defense.

VI

I went back to my teaching and to writing one-act pieces and a couple of volumes of short stories. Then I wrote two folk novels and occasionally took a hurried trip to Holly-wood to get money to pay for my house. But I couldn't give up my idea of symphonic drama. I thought to myself that if I had some place other than Broadway to try my theory out—some place where unions and rents and the implacable demand for profits could wait its season—maybe there I could possibly succeed.

Kurt Weill landed in this country about this time, a refu-gee from Hitler's fanaticism, and in 1936, with the encour-agement of the directors of the Group Theatre—Harold Clurman, Cheryl Crawford, and Lee Strasberg—he and I got together on a musical drama to be produced by the Group. I introduced some symphonic elements into my script, but it was in the main a straight music drama. Weill's score was splendid, but the public did not like the play. Perhaps the story line was faulty, and I suspect the subject matter was too. I had put into it a lot of my abhorrence of war and made Johnny Johnson, the leading character, a kindly common-sense man against whom and through whom I might measure the madness of violence and hate. Lee Strasberg did a good job of directing, and in the asylum scene especially, where Johnny had organized the League of World Republics on the pattern of the United States Senate, his work was sheer genius. Russell Collins played the lead, and among the cast were Robert Lewis, Roman Bohnen, Lee J. Cobb, Art Smith, Albert Van Dekker, Elia Kazan, John Garfield, Ruth Nelson, Paula Miller, Luther Adler, Morris Carnovsky, Tony Kraber, and others. The play limped along for three or four months and then closed.

Once more I went back to my teaching. The university

had been patient with me, giving me more than my share of leaves of absence over the years. And I kept writing stories and articles on the side. But still in my mind were the plan and hope to try out my ideas in a symphonic drama somewhere and somehow.

Such an opportunity came down in North Carolina the next year, when a group of local people decided to put on a celebration commemorating the three hundred and fiftieth anniversary of Sir Walter Raleigh's tragic attempts at a settlement on Roanoke Island down on the coast in the eastern part of the state. I got in with the group, and a play was planned. But we had little or no money. It was still the Depression and W.P.A. days, and finally the federal government helped us out. We got some funds, and contributions of labor and materials were made locally. So work began on an amphitheatre in which to produce the play. It was built on the exact spot by the sound's edge where Sir Walter Raleigh's colony had lived and died, and I set about writing the script.

And as always, let there be music, music on which the story might ride.

And then, before we could begin rehearsals our money ran out. With Professor Frederick H. Koch, who was a sort of inspiring guardian over the project, I went to a foundation in New York City for help—and got it.

We opened *The Lost Colony* on July 4, 1937, with Samuel Selden as director and Koch as advisory director, and although the nearest city was ninety miles away, it was a fair success from the start. We had some twelve or fifteen Federal Theatre Project actors in the main parts, many local actors in smaller parts, a chorus from the famous Westminster Choir College, and a swarm of C.C.C. camp boys as Indians. So the financial burden was relatively light. But everyone was paid something for his work. Our admission price was one dollar for adults and fifty cents for children, and with good crowds in an outdoor theatre seating thirty-two hundred we were able to pay our way. We got good write-ups from the leading critics. Atkinson, Garland, Kronenberger, and many others came down and gave us a boost. And the Cavalcade of America program carried a condensed nationwide hour-long radio broadcast. Then President Roosevelt came, and later Mrs. Roosevelt. The night the President saw the show we had to give two performances to accommodate the crowds. People were literally hanging in the old sprawled live-oak trees that surrounded the amphitheatre.

At last, I felt my theory of symphonic drama was vindicated. And with the exception of the blackout war years, the play has run a summer season of ten weeks each year since. Last summer marked its twentieth season, and soon it will pass its one thousandth performance. Hundreds of thousands of people have come to see this project of communal theatre—there on the yellow sands of Roanoke Island—come to hear the old English music, the folk songs and hymn tunes of our musical tradition, and to see the native Indian dances—all part of the symphonic drama that tells the story of a brave group of people, who in their struggle and death vindicated and made more living the ideals in which they believed and on which our nation is founded.

With *The Lost Colony* established, I looked around for other chances for symphonic outdoor productions. For by this time I had already decided that this sort of drama was exactly fitted to the needs and dramatic genius of the American people. There seemed to be something, too, about the outdoors that was native to our hearts and feelings. For we are a muscular, lithe, and bounding-footed people. Maybe it is the pioneer field, prairie, and forest influence still on us. And sitting under the stars at night and witnessing again plays that had to do with the making of this country maybe brought a sense of man and God and nature into one. Our richness of tradition, our imaginative folk life, our springing enthusiasm and health and drive, our singing and dancing and poetry, our lifted hearts and active feet and hands, even our outpourings of mechanical creations and things for self-expression—maybe in the outdoors and not in the professional and killingly expensive confines of the big cities, these could flourish and have their place.

And so I went to work with a will in writing other symphonic outdoor dramas to be produced in different parts of America—among them, *Big John* a Negro-spiritual drama for South Carolina, and *The Highland Call* for the Cape Fear River Scots. Then World War II came on, and all was stopped. I continued to teach, visit Hollywood now and then, and work on a novel. I wrote a straight play about education too, *The Enchanted Maze*, and with Richard Wright dramatized his intense novel, *Native Son*, which Orson Welles directed and produced in New York with much success.

After the war, Virginia decided she would like to have a play of *The Lost Colony* form also. And under the leadership of the former governor, Colgate W. Darden, money was raised, and a beautiful brick amphitheatre was built on the edge of the lake in the woods of the William and Mary campus at Williamsburg for the production of *The Common Glory*. In this play I told the story of Thomas Jefferson's struggles in helping to establish democratic government in the United States during the years 1775–81. Again I used with a free hand any and all elements of theatre art that I needed—music, dance, dreams, mental speech, battlefield scenes, warships in the river, and narration to drive the story along. Once more the same philanthropic organization up north encouraged us with a timely grant-in-aid. In spite of rain and storm and katydids in the trees, the play opened successfully in 1947 under the direction of Althea Hunt. Howard Scammon took over as director after Miss Hunt, and with Allen Matthews as manager, Myra Kinch as choreographer, Roger Sherman as technical director, and Sue Sherman as costumer, the production has improved summer after summer. Last season was the eleventh and I hope it will be running many years more.

Then Washington, D.C., decided to celebrate the one hundred and fiftieth anniversary of the setting up of the Federal Government there in 1800, and I began writing a drama for it. Immediately we ran into politics. The President of the United States came to our rescue with talks in our behalf, but politics continued. I spent more time lobbying and trying to raise funds from the Congress than I did on the play. And the script showed it. At last the huge amphitheatre in Rock Creek Park was completed at a cost of several hundred thousand dollars. We had everything one could ask for in lighting equipment, sound, dressing rooms, machinery, and shops. But the production didn't get across. I worked and sweated to do for George Washington what I had done for Sir Walter Raleigh's colony and for Jefferson, and the drama students from George Washington and Catholic universities did their valiant best for the play; but still our city audiences remained pretty skeptical and aloof. They were not impressed with my interpretation of the Father of Our Country, nor with the shadow-drama scenes and dream visions in the sky. However, I remember that Washington's crossing of the Delaware got a hand every night. We raised such a racket, too, in the Battle of Lexington scene that near-by irate householders flooded the papers with letters and even got out injunctions. After two seasons we closed up, and the multitude of lameduck souls and pie counter habitues who had been foisted on our pay-roll by the yea-saying congressmen and politicians had to seek sustenance elsewhere. It was all very sad, and for quite a while the thought of "symphonic outdoor drama" gave me the shudders. The only thing that eased my regrets was the knowledge that the city had received a fine civic out-door theatre for band and symphony concerts, musical productions, Boy Scout gatherings, sunrise Easter services, and other public uses.

VII

In 1951, the foundation that had twice helped my own plans asked me to go to Asia to lecture about art and litera-ture in the United States. I welcomed the chance. Not only would I be able to say to many groups and organizations that there was more in America than Yankee imperialism and scrambling for the dollar, but also I would have a chance to look at the theatre and dance-drama in different lands. It was a tough assignment, although I did not know how tough when I accepted. And so with my grant from the foundation and the blessings of UNESCO and the State Department, I set out. I managed to survive, and so did my wife, and I learned a lot. I first visited Honolulu and saw the indoor and outdoor theatres there and the great uni-versity collection of oriental drama. Then I went on to Japan, and no doubt that was the most fruitful part of my trip.

I do not have time in this account to tell much about the great Japanese theatre. It is already becoming well known in the United States through the recent writings of Faubion Bowers, Earle Ernst, James Michener, Joshua Logan, A. C. Scott, and others, and through such fine Japanese motion pictures as *Rashomon, Gate of Hell,* and *Ugetsu,* and through the visits of the Azuma dancers. But I found that in both the Noh and Kabuki dramas the Japanese were doing things on the stage—and had been doing them for one hundred years—that we were just beginning to do. Here indeed was the truly lyric and imaginative theatre so many of us yearning American playwrights had dreamed about. Here was the theatre in which were finally interwoven in proper proportions the various elements of dramatic imagination—music, dance, athletics, pantomime, choral chants, poetic narration and commentary, light and sound, and the impassioned actor's speech—all clothed in colorful costumes, settings, and the habiliments of the poet's dream.

I visited many other countries, made my lectures, and saw theatre in the Philippines, Malaya, Thailand, Burma, India, Turkey, Greece, and Italy, but nowhere did I see anything to equal what I saw in Japan.

It is my belief that in Kabuki, Japan has the finest production theatre in the world.

Back home I took up the symphonic outdoor drama idea again. Ohio was busy making plans for celebrating the one hundred and fiftieth anniversary of its statehood, and I was asked to write a play for that. I began work, and bills were introduced in the legislature to provide money for the production and for building an amphitheatre. The governor took a personal interest in it. One hundred thousand dollars was appropriated for the production, but the bill for the amphitheatre was killed. So we had to put the play on at the fairgrounds, and that meant that it had to be changed into more of a dramatic spectacle, a pageant, than a play. The areas were too vast, the distances too great for much straight story-telling. We used some five hundred actors in the production, two hundred dancers, a multitude of wagons and carts, horses and automobiles, choruses, an amplified orchestra, six narrators, Indians and soldiers, and in the finale a parade of the machine age as Ohio had contributed to it. As a "curtain" to end the spectacle, a coal-burning locomotive moved in along the race track from the right and a diesel locomotive in from the left to meet in front of the grandstand, while a huge chorus on the wide stage across the track sang Isaac Van Grove's patriotic anthem and a tremendous Ohio State flag descended from wires in the sky with spotlights flaring on it. We had audiences up to eleven thousand during the two-week run. The production was under the direction of Helen Geraghty.

In 1953, Berea College in the Kentucky foothills made plans for celebrating its 1955 centennial, and after getting off a little volume of essays about our dramatic heritage, I set to work on a symphonic outdoor drama for the event. The project was a challenging one from the very beginning. In the first place, I admired the kind of democratic education Berea College stood for, and in the second, I welcomed the chance to get at some of the beautiful, stored-up Appalachian folklore—ballad, song and dance—to put in my play. I soaked myself in the history of the Appalachian country and the Scotch-Irish people who had settled there. At last the imagined characters of the drama and their relationships were pulled into being, coming reluctantly forward to the stern demand of the drama's theme—creative education.

I made my imaginary hero, John Freeman, a blazing idealist and considered him inspired by John G. Fee and his associates. He had got himself some training at Berea and then at Oberlin College and finally come back into the mountains hoping to start a school among his people founded on the Berea ideal—an ideal expressed in the motto of that college—"For God hath made of one blood all nations of men for to dwell on all the face of the earth." Freeman's Scotch-Irish people lived in a narrow mountain valley and had lived there for two or three generations. Feuds were common among them. And many a young man in desperado activity had landed himself in an early grave or behind penitentiary bars, when with less ignorance and a little more learning he might have become a useful citizen. John Freeman had decided that education was the answer, and he went to work to prove it.

When he was a little boy, his father, a kindly mountain preacher, had been killed, say, by an exchange of shots when he stepped in between two angry groups of mountaineers in an effort to make peace. This tragedy had a profound effect on John. It helped him even in his early days to see the evil, the cruelty and waste of hate and bloodspilling, and it determined him in his heart never to take up a gun against his fellow man.

And there in his little mountain cabin he worked away at night, the fire flickering, worked at his books, his dreams, and his plans, studying and reading from his father's Bible, from American history, *Pilgrim's Progress*, and from many a book of sermons and poetry that he borrowed from the Berea library.

And he went forth preaching education and dedication of spirit in its name. He found some help in the mountain girl he loved, and he was always encouraged by his strong-hearted mother. Perhaps the task John Freeman set himself could not be accomplished, for it was nothing short of trying to teach and put into practice the Christian faith in which he believed.

As ye know, so shall ye do, he said, and as a man thinketh in his heart, so is he.

He soon ran into difficulties. Old ways do not change easily. Old beliefs are not broken in a day, and the Scotch-Irish people in that valley were a hardy, stubborn lot. And

John was stubborn too. Like St. Paul, he had seen the vision. He would not give over.

Then murmurings and suspicions began to rise against him. The threat of the Civil War grew darker over the land, and his pro-Southern neighbors found themselves more and more outraged by his beliefs. He was against slavery and said so. He was for the Union, and he declared it. He was against guns and killings, whatever the cause, and he kept speaking this conviction. And then, perhaps worst of all, he advocated education of the Negroes and giving them a chance to grow and to develop their lives. And day after day in his little school he stood up and taught these beliefs to his students.

The threats against him finally became a fact, and the brutish feet of force swept over him and his work. But he was a fighter, too—not with swords and bayonets and bullets, but with words and ideas and with love. And although his neighbors came in the night and burned down his school, he would not strike back with his fist, he would not hate the misguided hand that had furnished the torch. But he would go on preaching his ideas—preaching from the church, from the crossroads, the country store, wherever he could find a listener. And when he was dragged out and beaten, he still kept his faith, his determination. And while the blood ran down his stricken shoulders, he cried out, "I'll never give in to them. In God's name my flesh will be stronger than their steel."

Then when the Confederate forces overran Kentucky, and he saw the nation he loved about to break in two and slavery and oppression continue, he was faced with the dilemma of remaining a follower of his pacifist religion or taking up his gun and fighting for the cause he believed in. He prayed and agonized over this decision, and in a scene at night on the mountain top he communed with the spirit of his dead father. From the void beyond the crags the voice of old Luke Freeman spoke again to him the ancient and homely mysterious doctrine of a man saving his life by losing it.

Out of his Golgotha experience John Freeman thought that he glimpsed the nature of sacrifice—the implacable demand that an ideal always makes of its followers in the crisis hour—and the crisis hour must always come if the ideal is to live—a demand that he, the believer, must offer up what he holds dearest and most precious to prove his faith, prove it not only to himself but to those who must to their human eyes have that proof. And laying aside his Bible, he picked up his gun and marched away to war. And there in the smoke and yelling fury of battle he led his Federal troops against his Southern neighbors, among whom was his own brother—led them to victory and to his own death.

At the end of the play, with the fighting done and the Blue and Gray united in a common sorrow, the people in the valley brought John Freeman's body home again and above his open grave promised one another to build his school.

John Freeman's teachings would go on.

Under the leadership of Dr. W. D. Weatherford of the Berea board of trustees, and President Francis S. Hutchins, a charming amphitheatre of native stone was built for the play there among the Kentucky hills some three miles from the campus. It was decided to limit the seating capacity to some eighteen hundred, as compared with twenty-five hundred or three thousand in the others. For I had found it hard to put across vivid and intimate scenes in the larger ones. And more often than not pageantry and crowd gatherings had been necessary to subdue the outdoor environment when the uncluttered story itself was what counted most. Gestures had to be broad and definite, exaggeratedly so, and the speech more often of a declamatory kind than not. The individualization of the characters had to be done in a few broad strokes, and most often a narrator or interpretative voice was required to keep the story cleaned up and running to the point, so that the audience could receive the full impact of the play without too much waste on explanatory matters.

In this smaller theatre I was able to remedy some of these defects and realize a more intense drama than before. The results proved the wisdom of our decision, and with an average ticket price of $1.80, a seating capacity of this size could still support a weekly payroll of several thousand dollars and leave something over for a sustaining fund.

With Samuel Selden directing, *Wilderness Road* opened on June 29, 1955, for its first summer season. The reviews were good in all the local papers, as well as in *The New York Times* and *Herald Tribune*, although some of the critics made a point of "the inflammable nature of the play." The people liked the folk singing and dancing, the flags and waving banners, bugles and drums and marching feet—all an integral part of the story—but they liked most the inner drama of John Freeman's struggle to make the ideas he believed in prevail. The play now seems set for a run of many years.

This type of drama, which I have elected to call "symphonic," seems to be catching on throughout the country, especially when the productions are outdoors and the subject matter is historical. Samuel Selden, head of the drama department at the University of North Carolina, has been one of the most consistent and pioneer workers in it. Also Kermit Hunter, Harry Davis, John Parker, Foster Fitz-Simons, Kai Jurgenson, and Irene Smart—all of that university—are helping to spread it into a movement. They have cooperated on such projects not only in North Carolina and Kentucky but in Illinois, Tennessee, and Florida. And other similar undertakings are now in the making in Georgia, Indiana, California, Pennsylvania, and Massachusetts. Kermit Hunter's outdoor play *Unto These Hills*, which he calls a "saga" drama and not "symphonic," is one of the most popular of them all. It plays every summer at Cherokee, North Carolina, in a lofty mountainside amphitheatre built for its production in 1951. Hunter has written a number of these plays, and his *Horn in the West* is also acted annually at Boone, North Carolina. During the year 1956 he opened another one, *Chucky Jack*, at Gatlinburg, Tennessee, and in 1957 his experiment in religious drama, *Thy Kingdom Come*, was played at Salem, Virginia.

Another pioneer group working in the symphonic outdoor drama is at Williamsburg, Virginia, most of its members being from the faculty of the College of William and Mary. Up to the time of his death last year Allen Matthews was its imaginative and beloved leader, having as his associates Howard Scammon, Myra Kinch, Althea Hunt, Roger and Sue Sherman, Carl Fehr, Al Haak, Anthony Manzi, Harold Chapman, and Rachel Hitchens. They have produced *The Common Glory* there at Williamsburg for the past eleven seasons, and in 1957 they added *The Founders*, the Jamestown play which I had long planned and at last finished for Virginia's festival year. A second amphitheatre was built near *The Common Glory* one for the production of this play, the former play running in the afternoon and the latter in the evening. Due to the 1957 success of the two dramas, it is planned to continue the dual presentation year after year.

VIII

So great is the demand becoming for this type of drama that new playwrights, directors, and technicians now need to be recruited. I think the drama departments in the different colleges and universities could well turn their attention to training their young people for this work—as well as for Broadway. It is still in its infancy. And I do not think that it is too much to hope that other playwrights, directors, actors, and workers to come some day will somehow perfect this form, and every American city of any size will have its neighboring amphitheatre, where plays derived out of the people's lives and their history, as well as from other sources, will have continuing productions. Then—who knows?—we may have begun to create an American dramatic art comparable to that of the ancient Greeks, when Aeschylus and Sophocles walked the earth and spoke lifting words beneath the bending sky for all to hear.

Well, as Granowsky said, there is much, much to be done.

Drama and the Weather

A Letter in Reply to the Editor of *Theatre Arts*

If you've ever been down in the country during a severe summer drought, you have noticed how the crops stood lifeless and how the leaves and limbs of the trees sagged under the wilting heat, and how the chickens in the barnyard sat slothfully on the ground, and the cattle in the shadow of the buildings looked out at the world with dull and inert eyes. The farmers themselves seemed testy and irritable about the house, and with reason, for day after day the sun has risen like a ball of fire, swum across the brazen empty sky and gone down beyond the rim of brown hills—a fiery curse to animal, earth, and man. The world itself is perishing for rain, but there is no rain.

Then one morning a different feeling is in the air. After breakfast you walk in the lane, and a change is over everything. The flowers and the trees have perked up their heads, the chickens step about lively, and the pigeons no longer quarrel under the eaves. Down in the pasture the cattle move briskly around biting off green willow tips, and the farmer and his sons are long ago abroad looking to their dikes and ditches. You go down to the village for the mail. More than once you hear a store loafer say, "The air feels like rain." Being a summer boarder, you read the morning papers, then an article or two in a magazine about trouble in Europe, and after lunch sit on the front porch and take a rest.

Looking off across the burning fields about two o'clock, you see low on the horizon edge a faint little wad of cloud, no larger than the cloud Elijah or Polonius saw. And as you sit there watching, another little cloud appears swimming up the sky, to be followed by another and then another. Soon the whole southwestern horizon is marked by these little upboiling racks. And in less time than it takes to tell, a low dark swollen band begins shoving itself up behind them and above the line of sycamore trees along the river. Presently there is a roll of low ominous thunder below the earth, and the windows rattle in their sockets.

The moments pass, the dark wide stretching cloud now reaches from north to south and pushes up until it touches the edge of the burning sun. Then it obscures the sun. A flash of lightning marks a sudden fiery crack from sky to earth. The elm trees around the house shiver with a strange delight. The chickens start going into the henhouse and the doves fly into their cote. And then up from the meadow the old bell-cow comes leading the other cattle, her head high, her tail arched merrily.

Another roll of thunder sounds, a gust of dust cuts a little jigging whirlwind swift down the lane, trying to keep up with the edge of the cloud which now has raced across the sky and passed over the house. The wind blows more strongly, and somewhere a door slams. You continue to sit, waiting for the rain to fall. The wind dies out, the thunder is no longer heard, nor is there any lightning. Everything is breathless, expectant, still.

Now with a sudden clatter like stones on the roof or gravel thrown, the rain begins. A fine mist of dust is beat up in the yard, and in the lane and out across the fields. Like a morning ground-fog it is. And then it too is wetted down to earth as the rain settles into a steady pour. A sheet of wetness begins to blow in on you, and the air is full of a rich sodden, loamy smell. You pick up your chair, lean it against the wall, and enter the house. There you stand by the window looking out where a world is being refreshed and where a snake of yellow water has started wriggling down the dry road ditch. The drought is over. In a few days everything will be green again.

There was once an old question as to who could chart the winds and the nature thereof, and who could foretell the weather and its whims. The question still stands today unanswered as it did in Job's time. No doubt there are laws governing all such phenomena, and maybe someday these laws will be understood—laws that have no irrational phantom dancing within them. But even so those who understand will have little power to bring either drought or rain, for the wind will still blow where it listeth, and in the universe at large it will rain when it will rain.

And as with the weather, so with writing a play—so with any work of art. It comes pretty much when it will come, is absent when it will be absent, and no man can provide its presence at his will. So if I may be personal in replying to your question, "Why do you write plays," I can on first consideration easily say, "I don't know." It is much like the weather to me—the what and why, the wherefore and results. About the only answer I would venture is that I seem to need to. If I were certain that the drama were the one means of gaining honor or wealth or mental stability, there would be some obvious sense in spending one's life trying to set down lines for people to speak on a stage. I believe I should want to write plays, though, if little or nothing came of them, but naturally I want a lot to come of them.

Of course your question goes further than any easy answer or any meteorological metaphor. It raises the whole

problem of aptitude and calling. I think all people are by
nature artists, that is, more or less so. The usual European
designation of the American builder and business man as a
money hog, for instance—a creature who takes pleasure
only in dollar profit and pain only in dollar loss—seems to
me obviously false. There is more to it than that—always
more. Sinclair Lewis in one of his novels, *Work of Art*,
tries his hand at showing that one Myron Weagle with his
dream of a perfect hotel might be considered essentially an
artist. There is a lot of human truth in his contention. Now
if all of us have this so-called artistic urge, then why do
some of us become hotel-keepers and others banjo-pickers
or playwrights? That is the next question. The answer is
perhaps that circumstances always play their part. One child
happens to have access, say, to a piano near at hand but finds
his fingers too stiff or too short ever to allow of his becoming a performer. Perhaps he turns to composing, or brick-
laying. And so it goes. Each of us could make some sort of
statement as to his proper calling. Take your own case—
you run a drama magazine. All sorts of odds and ends of
circumstances and people went into your choice of that
career.

Two incidents happened to me years ago, I remember,
which turned me to writing plays. Norman Foerster, who
was one of the finest English teachers ever to appear at the
University of North Carolina, announced in class one day
that the seniors had decided to do a play at Commencement
and were holding a contest for original scripts. He advised
me to try my hand. I took a chance at the thing and happened to win out. The play was produced in the forest
theatre and I was thrilled to death. After that though I
didn't set my heart on playwriting, for I had always been
more interested in poetry and short stories than anything
else. Then in 1919 "Proff" Koch came riding in from the
Dakota prairies, his arms full of plays and his head full of

dreams. In no time a stage was up, and everybody near and far, little and big, black and white, realized for the first time that he, said body, was an artist of some sort—mainly a dramatic artist. Some went in for designing, some for acting, some for writing. I chose the last. And after a few productions, I was caught fast in my choice and had struck acquaintance with all the bat-like terrors that inhabit the shadows of the stage.

Your next question is easier to answer. "Why do you write the plays you do?" The answer is—that's the only kind I know how to write. Most of the plays I have written can be designated as folk plays, and I know this seems a narrow boundary. Perhaps it is, but since the "folk" are the people who seem to matter most to me, I have little interest in trying to deal with others who are more foreign and therefore less real to me. Not for a moment do I claim to have done justice to an inspiring subject matter, but the challenge is there, clearer, sharper, and more compelling every day. For there is something in the life of "the people" which seems of deeper significance so far as the nature of the universe goes than the characters who might be termed sophisticated. To examine the matter a little further, it seems to me that the folk are those living closer to a terrible and all-wise nature than their brethren of the sidewalks and opera house, and if I were seeking a philosophical statement for the matter it would be somewhat as follows:

The folk are the people whose manners, ethics, religious and philosophical ideals are more nearly derived from and controlled by the ways of the outside physical world (Cf. Synge's *Riders to the Sea*) than by the ways and institutions of men in a specialized society (Cf. Schnitzler's *Anatol* cycle). And the outside natural world is the fountain of wisdom, the home of the fruitful all-mother, the omnipotent God. The line of demarcation between the folk and sophisticated drama is not always easily contrasted; to in-

stance once more, Ferenc Molnar's *The Guardsman* and
S. Ansky's *The Dybbuk*. And between the last two I'd
always choose *The Dybbuk*—even though technique should
shift for itself.

I don't claim that sophisticated drama may not be great
in its own right, but somehow I never thrill to it as I do
to what I like to term the folk drama the Greeks wrote,
the kind Shakespeare and Tolstoy and Hauptmann wrote;
the kind Alexis Granowsky used to produce in Russia with
its lovely burden of folk-imagery, music and song. In
reading *Lear,* for example, I always feel a sudden lift when
we come to the heath scene. There is something grand
and universal in the naked relationship of the old king to
the powers of nature and the weather around him.

And as characters available to art purposes, to repeat,
those who live as it were with their feet in the earth and
their heads bare to the storms, the lightning and the gale
—those who labor with their hands, wrestling from cryptic
nature her goods and stores of sustenance—these develop a
wisdom of living which seems to me more real and beautiful
than those who develop their values and ambitions from
rubbing shoulders in a crowded city.

And that wisdom it is which seems important—a wisdom
which is a consciousness of the great eternal Presence by
which men live and move and have their being, and without which they die. And if the playwrights who tell of
captains and lords, kings and queens, dolls and manikins,
can open up the doors of crowded buildings, cut through
the filmy arras that conceals our human instincts and hopes
and fears, and go to the first principles of human identity
—then they raise the hair on our heads too with their voice
from the sacred grove of Colonus. And no longer do we
think of man as sophisticated or folk, but man—man alone
with his God and his destiny. And when this happens—

and rare is Shakespeare, rarer than the Phoenix—then the matter is all one and listeners are all one.

But the present clang and confusion of wheel on iron, yelling and clamor of tickers and tellers, the secrecy of vaults and locks and braggarty monoliths of incorruptible concrete and steel—these all make it harder for us to see and hear the God who is the principle of our lives. (Not God, a supernatural personality sitting on a foolish throne in heaven. No, no! But the Principle of worship, of reverence, of awe—the primal Verity native to the soul.) Maybe I'm crazy on the idea of God, but then aren't we all? I refer to the wild pell-mell rush every evening out of the city to the country—to the country where the birds are, where the grass is, and where there is peace or should be.

Now you catch me almost carrying on into a scheme of social philosophy. And if I wanted to apply this half-surmised aesthetic theory to the control and arrangement of peoples, I should say there ought to be plenty of trees and land and outdoors for every man. For only in the outdoors can we associate with power and mystery in their most sublime manifestation. And heaven knows we ought to sense in any way we can whatever touch of sublimity there may be vouchsafed unto us in this darkness.

Now it seems that after all I'm saying for myself that folk-drama as such is or can be more significant than sophisticated drama. Not at all. I mean to repeat that in the last analysis it is a question of neither folk nor sophisticate—but of man, man in his environment, and it is in the main a matter for the poet, the creator, the seer. And I would say that indoors sooner or later man must perish and outdoors there is more of a chance for him.

To make another dogmatic statement, I would say that cruelty, scorn, and evils of all sorts are more native to the great cities than not, and therefore we should be better off without any great cities—I mean close, skyscraper, bedlam cities. (There's something other than politics behind Russia's efforts to create the ideal commune.) And all the little towns that get too large for their britches and so full of metropolital urges and apings that they cut down all the trees on their main streets and cover the grass and ground with concrete, will be better off when they tear up the concrete, reset the trees, and grow grass again. And maybe now that we have evolved wheels and telephones and radios and machinery of long-distance cooperation of all sorts, we can all begin to live more among flowers and trees again and yet keep in touch with each other enough for our sophisticated needs. Then haply now and again we may also have a word with the Great Presence where He walks by the river bank at evening.

As to your next question of "What happens when you turn your play over to the director, designer, actor, and see them add their form to yours?"—it is more than easy to say that sometimes you are pleased with what they do and sometimes disappointed. It is never possible for the image-picture of your characters to be entirely duplicated on the stage. Their habits, their actions and appearance are always different and necessarily so. But I think the production as often improves the play over the author's mind as it is likely to hurt it—that is, a good production.

Your last question as to what the playwright should be to the theatre and to the world he lives in, opens up a huge wheel-full of diverging thoughts. Briefly though, he should be, don't you think, the same to the theatre as the gardener to his garden, or the blacksmith to his smithy, and the carpenter to his house? And as for the world he lives in—his business is simply to express in dramatic form the human struggles, both evil and good, that exist in that world. In the Aristotelian phrase, he is a maker, and his business is to fashion or make his material fit the imaginative demands of his craft. But how wonderfully difficult it is and how joyful! How like the weather, like the rain!

And in these two words of material and craft all the trouble lies, of course. But the trouble is not final, however mysterious and difficult the matter is—do you think so? For in the great outside universe around us nature is always solving these dualistic antagonisms, whether it be raining or whether it be dry, and from her we may no doubt derive both the axiom and the dream.

It occurs to me that I make no place for comedy (which includes melodrama and farce). Well, it apparently belongs to another point of view, just as the grotesque requires still a third kind of judgment. Comedy seeks to belong entirely to man's world and to have no place in nature's world. In fact one might say that it arises from man's delight in prankishness with himself and fellowman in so far as he forgets that he is a part of an all-powerful and demanding universe. Its basic pattern is a non-harmful incongruity which man himself provides, and that would seem to justify the definition. For nature is never funny or playful, not even when she smiles, is she?

As for the grotesque (the hysterical), it disappears before definition and stands representative of nothing more than the frightful effort to combine the comic and the sublime (or the finite funny with the infinite serious) into the body of one piece.

You see, your letter has stirred up a whole hornet's nest of trouble for me. And now that I've had to take refuge in the quagmire of metaphysics, I'd better stop. So I'll conclude by—yes, I'll say it—the play's the thing after all, whether it's indoors or outdoors—but like the weather it is most outdoors.

On the Democratic Ideal

What is this democratic ideal of ours?

It is a vision, an intuition of a nation, of a world of free and self-reliant men—men of good will, of courage, of truth and justice. It is a philosophy of government which declares that each individual of whatever race, color, creed or calling has a right as well as a duty to his fullest self-development and the exercise of his talents as becomes the dignity and worth of a man.

It is an ideal then of self-government—of liberty and rights and a compelling responsibility to these liberties and rights.

The ideal began long ago. It appeared for a while in the glory that was Greece. It was put forth in fervent and dramatic terms in the life and character of Jesus Christ and the New Testament. A fragment of its shape showed itself in the Magna Carta in the words saying, "to no man will we deny or delay right or justice." And in the first legislative assembly in the New World at Jamestown in 1619 it was seeking a restatement and social practice when the burgesses met "to make, ordain, and establish all manner of orders, laws, directives, instructions, forms and ceremonies of government and magistracy fit and necessary for and concerning the government of this colony." And in the Mayflower Compact of our hardy Pilgrims it was still further and outwardly defined when they covenanted "to enact, constitute and frame such just and equal laws, ordinances, acts, constitutions, offices from time to time as shall be thought most meet and convenient for the general good of the colony: under which we promise all due submission and obedience."

And once more in the English Bill of Rights, and in the writings of the Englishman, John Locke, and of the Frenchman, Jean Jacques Rousseau, these same principles of human conduct and inspiration were embodied and kept in breath and alive.

And more familiarly to us the idea was interpreted and affirmed by George Mason in his 1776 Virginia Declaration of Rights, and by that dedicated libertarian and moral thinker, Thomas Jefferson, who in the Declaration of Independence at the beginning of our young nation's life maintained that we Americans "hold these truths to be self-evident—that all men are created equal, that they are endowed by their Creator with certain unalienable rights —that among these are life, liberty and the pursuit of happiness. That to secure these rights, governments are instituted among men, deriving their just powers from the consent of the governed."

The right to happiness! Their just powers! The consent of the governed! These true and blazing words—as deep as time and as simple, as richly invigorating and full of hope as the beckoning far horizon.

And in his *Common Sense* the tough and eloquent Thomas Paine declared the same, saying further too that "the cause of America is in great measure the cause of all mankind."

And again and again this same Thomas Jefferson discerned the bright lineaments of the American ideal, asserting that "truth is great and will prevail—that she is the proper and sufficient antagonist to error and has nothing to fear from the conflict unless by human interposition disarmed of her natural weapons—free argument and debate, errors ceasing to be dangerous when it is permitted freely to contradict them."

The one certain defence against untruth being truth. Against error to oppose the right. Against all evil to put forward the good. Not by arms alone shall the palm of victory be won. For it is in the hearts and minds of men that the city is taken or made safe! And not once but many times George Washington, the first founder of our new republic, spoke his courageous words, his devotion and faith for us all. In his famous letter to the governors of the separate states—alas not famous enough, not well-known enough in our schoolrooms especially—at the end of the Revolution he reiterated his devotion to the American ideal:

"I now make it my earnest prayer that God would have you and the state over which you preside in His holy protection; that He would incline the hearts of the citizens to cultivate a spirit of subordination and obedience to government; to entertain a brotherly affection and love for one another, for their fellow citizens of the United States at large, and particularly for their brethren who have served in the field; and finally, that He would most graciously be pleased to dispose us all to do justice, to love mercy, and to demean ourselves with that charity, humility, and pacific temper of mind, which were the characteristics of the Divine Author of our blessed religion, and without an humble imitation of those examples in these things, we can never hope to be a happy nation."

Justice, mercy, charity, humility and peace! A nation grounded in the principles of truth and religion!

And again in his Farewell Address this strong-hearted and good man adjures us, you and me and our children's children, to remember that "of all the dispositions and habits which lead to political prosperity, religion and morality are indispensable supports. In vain would that man claim the tribute of patriotism who should labor to subvert these great pillars of human happiness, these firmest props of the duties of Men and Citizens."

And further in the same address he continues with reasoned and candid earnestness— "Observe good faith and justice towards all Nations. Cultivate peace and harmony with all. Religion and morality enjoin this conduct; and can it be that good policy does not equally enjoin it? It will be worthy of a free, enlightened, and at no distant period a great nation to give to mankind the magnanimous and too novel example of a people always guided by an exalted justice and benevolence. Who can doubt that in the course of time and things, the fruits of such a plan would richly repay any temporary advantages which might be lost by a steady adherence to it? Can it be, that Providence has not connected the permanent felicity of a nation with its virtue? The experiment, at least, is recommended by every sentiment which ennobles human nature."

And in a letter written by Warden Seixas of the Hebrew Congregation in Newport, Rhode Island, to General Washington in 1790—this leader among his Jewish people declared his devotion to this American vision, saying of the new government that he and his people found it offered "to bigotry no sanction, to persecution no assistance, but generously affording to all liberty of conscience and immunities of citizenship, deeming everyone of whatever nation, tongue or language equal parts of the great Government machine. This so ample and extensive union whose basis is philanthropy, mutual confidence and public virtue, we cannot but acknowledge to be the work of the great

God who ruleth in the armies of heaven and among the inhabitants of the earth, doing whatever seemeth Him good."

Again and again through the documents of these our founding fathers and statesmen we find this summons, this challenge—this plea for liberty of conscience, for morality, for good will, and always the admonition to responsibility and "public virtue."

And finally in one grand summation our Constitution itself rededicates us to these principles of the ideal—freedom of religion, of speech, of the press, of the right of the people peaceably to assemble and to petition the government for a redress of their grievances, security of a man in his person and property, due process of law, habeas corpus, trial by jury, and freedom from slavery and servitude, as becomes a reliant and courageous people.

Old, old words, but ever new, ever fresh in their rightness and their meaning.

These are the constituents, the elements of moral and social strength then, the truths that go into the making of our philosophy of government—the true doctrine out of which our political faith has taken shape and grown.

In defense of these principles a horrible and degrading Civil War was fought and won. Abraham Lincoln lost his life, a sacrifice in their behalf, and the great Robert E. Lee, serving these principles as he felt them to be, plunged his own life down to tragedy and pain. And Woodrow Wilson and likewise thousands of other men have given their all that the right should prevail.

For this is a religion, this faith of ours. It is of the spirit then, and with the spirit it must be served.

Or it will perish.

And as a spiritual way of life it is opposed unalterably

to that other religion known as dialectical materialism or Marxism, or of most recent days, as Communism.

For the ideal of our self-government conceives of each individual as a unit of absolute and prime value in himself. It maintains that he precedes the group, the institution, the state even, and continues and endures beyond them. His value is that of a human immortal soul, with its own sanctity and inviolability against any and all authoritarian abuse and tyranny whatsoever.

In this concept of a man's worth and his behaving, the American faith, the American way of life, then, is one with the basic truths of Christianity. And in times of stress the church militant is the church alive.

The present hour cries out for democracy militant, democracy as a religion alive! So we must be up and doing. We must strive harder now than ever to amend our failures, our weakness, to get rid of our injustices, our racial abuses. We must look about us and weed out the evils that have too long infested the temple of our truth. These evils still meet us everywhere we turn. The regenerating, revitalizing of our democratic way of life must begin with each in-dividual, with you and me. It is not to be done through the group, through the state or through rulings of the church, or any institution, for that matter. They can help, but only help. It must creatively begin here in the heart with each of us.

You cannot fight ideas with bullets.

We must not wait for the voice of an opposing way of life to clamor forth the weaknesses in our own. We must dis-cover them for ourselves, must cure them ourselves.

In this crisis of a divided world we are spending billions on fantastic and frightening armaments. It seems we can-not do otherwise—seems, I say. But this I know—and I learned it from our founding fathers—that unless our nation also keeps itself armed in its heart, soul and mind with the eternal truths of its religion, of its righteous ideal, then all armaments and weapons of defense and offense whatsoever will ultimately be in vain. And the glory that might have been ours will have passed away. The America that was to be will not have been. And we who took up the sword and relied on it shall have perished by the sword.

The ideal without the idealist dies.

The Artist's Challenge

I

The ideal of the beautiful has ceaselessly haunted the human race, and man through the ages has sought to fashion his life in terms of that ideal. But betrayed by his own appetites, weakened and confused by false doctrines, a prey to imagined ills and nightmares of dread, and hindered and handicapped by many an evil chance and accident of fortune and war, he has too often failed in this seeking and too rarely succeeded. But still his effort to build an ever more noble life goes on, and will go on until the scientific universe has swallowed him and his dream to nothingness, or until he has won something of his final and ultimate victory. The eventuality of the former is the business of omnipotent and necessitous nature, but the possibility of the latter, imagined or otherwise, is all his concern and his alone. In this his destiny as a man is fixed, and to yield up the struggle like a clod or complacent animal is to invite the death in which there is no dream of resurrection.

By the very nature of his being, man is a living soul and not all animal. The first act of thinking is to declare it. And as a living soul, a spirit, he is a creator, a maker, an artist. His life itself is an effort in creation. From his birth to his death he shapes fair forms where there were none. He makes his songs even in tongueless silence, and builds his

shining structures among the wayward sticks and stones—
even from these sticks and stones. He begets life in the
midst of death, and as a prophet sings of hope among the
omens of doom. So does he forever try to find and fashion
forth that ideal of perfection which haunts him from the
cradle to the grave. So does he endlessly create new
products of that ideal, being himself a new creation beyond
all accounting-for out of time and space, and in his intent
like the idealized Power itself that first created him. And
he carries in his heart the divine imperative of this his
Maker's will by which he came. This is once more his glory
and vindication for being born, this the rich rewarding for
the enthralling burden, the tragic and comic venture of his
days.

And down the stretchy path of history behind him, he
has left the tokens and witnesses of this fact. Many a
temple, tomb, shrine, book, picture, song, statue, bridge,
road, or invention, he has reared in proud and ecstatic
affirmation of the findings on his noble quest. And here
and there, however far apart they be, have been ages,
periods of time when the inspiration of the ideal has seized
upon and fired him, not separate and alone, but in whole
communities and groups of men alike. And the single
prophetic voice, the single pair of valiant hands, have been
joined by other voices and other pairs of hands, and a
mighty concerted effort of creation set to work. Then it
was, those cultures and bodies of corporate beauty were
erected which still remain to us, living and real and un-
corrupted by corroding time. Through them the past was
made manifest in meaning, and the future had its hope. In
any roll call today they still declare their truth and glory.

II

The Chaldean seers, brooding on the wide, inscrutable sky, found in the mystic signs and configurations written in the stars a message of care and purpose for the human race. And in their records of clay and stone they put their readings down, and for generations men were gladdened and encouraged on their way because of them. The Egyptian builders with their pyramids and ponderous temples glimpsed the eternality of life that lives through and beyond death, and they avowed their buoyant hope even in the grave, even in the tokens of the scented cerement, the mummy, and the bull. And the sages and poets of China, out of darkness, flood, and hunger, envisioned the kingdom celestial and radiant on high and man's citizenship in that kingdom. The Brahmin gazed upon the everlasting blindness and emptiness of space and found not death there but a principle of fertility and beneficence to man. And he sang it forth in his divine books for us to draw comfort from—the *Vedas* and *Upanishads*.

The Persians, too, witnessed the weary round of the setting sun and the falling night, and discovered not frustration and hopelessness in that iteration but the logic of man's soul ever renewing itself in light unquenchable, a mystery to be celebrated and adored. The Buddhists in their ceaseless search through the tangle of sin and pain arrived at the eight-fold way and the soul's peace in worshipful contemplation along that way. The Jewish wanderer through long wilderness trials and sufferings finally found his abiding place in Canaan Land, and in thanksgiving and praise avowed his Lord of Hosts above, who reigned in majesty and glory and whose beauty was like the eyelids of the morning. And the maligned and beaten Jesus and his disciples, treading the sharp shards of Golgotha, sang above their bleeding feet of the gift of love and humility of men. The Greek in his rocky and arid hills created the fable of the dawn-beautiful world of grace and symmetry, of measure and balance, where luminous men and women, gods and goddesses, walked in his own ideal of the beautiful, the noble, and the true. The knight of the middle ages, burning with the vision of the shining grail, rode to face death and all unimaginable terrors in demon-infested forests, ogre-haunted caverns and mountains, as he strove to find the emblem of his yearning and bring it home.

And in Elizabethan England, Shakespeare and his fellows sang in lyric poems and plays of the wonder of a new-awakened age, the glory of far empires and adventures of strong imaginative men ruling and exploring the earth and marking out its boundaries, and the sublimity of the moral order over them and in them. The poet-scientists then in this same England found the law which asserted that the smallest and dullest fragment of matter, the ultimate point of space, and the last instant of time, are not soulless and inchoate things but are permeated by the universal relationship and meaning of the whole. Nothing is excepted whether of matter, space, or time, they said, and all that exists is beholden to this power, is haunted by the ideal of harmony and beauty.

And in that rich musical century in Germany, the creative spirit of man working in Bach, Mozart, and Beethoven sang forth as never before or since its hymns and dithyrambs, its melody and harmony, telling of the hopes and dreams of the human race and the ideal of beauty and the perfect order. And even in the natural world of physical vitality itself, Darwin, Wallace, Huxley, and Spencer broke the riddle open and found again this same ideal of perfection and upward climb at work, a self-improvement moving toward the ever-beckoning goal—however bloody and red the gory way.

So the story has gone.

III

These have been some of the great ages, the mountain peaks of man's experience and his effort. And though many a wide valley of desolation and dry bones may lie between, it is only the mountain peaks that mark for us the geography of that wide discovered land, it is only they our imagination ranges and feeds among, and they alone as it were which give forth oracular tongues to speak to us of inspiration and the dream. The rest is silence and forgetfulness. And on these mountain tops the beacon fires lighted long ago by vanished hands still burn for us. And as they illumine the darkness of the past so do they cast their gleam a little way along the path we have to go and where we too shall build our mountain peaks and light our fires as witnesses to the creative spirit for those that shall come after us—where we shall build them if we will.

In each of these times and deeds of accomplishments the adjurement and the theme have always been the same—man in search of his ideal. The inner voice speaks it clear for all to hear, echoes the truth that lives in all men's souls—saying: "In the beginning was the Word, and the Word was with God, and the Word was God. The same was in the beginning with God. . . . And the Word was made flesh, and dwelt among us, and we beheld his glory, the glory as of the only begotten of the Father, full of grace and truth." And when an age, an individual, have ceased to listen to this voice, have weakened in the search, given over the divine prerogative and yielded to sloth and fatness of days, to despair or denial, they have perished without exception and with no memorial of meaning to tell that they had been.

The poets and the prophets, the singers, the rightful builders and the priests have repeated this theme from generation to generation. For there is no other real theme to repeat and should be none. With Plato they have said: "Man must learn to use the beauties of earth as steps along which he mounts upward, going from fair forms to fair practices, and from fair practices to fair notions, until from fair notions he arrives at the notion of absolute beauty, and at last knows what the essence of beauty is. . . . If man has eyes to see the true beauty, he becomes the friend of God and immortal." With Hegel they reiterate that "Art and the creation of art, being works which originate in and are begotten of the spirit, are themselves stamped with the hallmark of spirit."

And with a fervid Nietzsche they assert: "Art is essentially affirmation, benediction, deification of existence. The artist's function is the invention and arrangement of a world in which we affirm ourselves in our inmost needs. The artist makes artists of all who can appreciate his message. Works of art arouse the condition which creates art." And with Eugene Veron they declare: "Art, from being the blossom and fruit of civilization, is rather its germ. . . . Art is the direct and spontaneous manifestation of human personality." And so on.

IV

Such is the doctrine of man the idealist, of man the artist and creator. And even in this present hour when the followers of brutal might and the iron fist are abroad in the world declaring otherwise, we are the more certain of its truth. For it is a proof of the blindness and degradation of these men, whatever their nationality, that they offer force instead of love, the fist instead of the friendly enclosing hand. From the boneyard of their confusion and greed they proclaim that "Ideas such as democracy, conscience of the world, internationality of art, breed cowardice." From their puppet podiums they shout that by strength of national arms a new world will be built by these fresh hands. In their folly they denounce as weaknesses the virtues that normal healthy-minded men instinctively crave everywhere—kindliness, brotherhood, love for one another, mutual kinship, as aspiring beings seeking for the same perfection and traveling down the same long way together, irrespective of race or creed.

For the fanatics and their half-mad followers, such principles as these are but sickly phantasms of a superstitious and outmoded time, and are to be destroyed, will be destroyed whenever and wherever they meet the triumphant march of the sons of force. So they say and continue to say even as their undoing draws quickly on, even as the grotesque impedance they would seek to lay across the path of progress is being shouldered away by a buoyant and healthy-minded people.

This is the old story of man's frailty and his failure. There have been other tyrannies and other hordes of heavy-footed men in other ages who have tried to flout the everlasting truth by which the world lives and has its being. They have often for a while succeeded in disrupting the fated flow and will of things, but not for long. And as they substitute the sword and the rifle for the Bible and the song, just so in the end do these same instruments render a mocking requiem over them. And the only light to shine above their wordless grave today is shed from those same beacon fires they in their madness so futilely tried to quench.

For it is an obvious thing that power and force, armies raised and battles fought, speeches declaimed and practices indulged in, are useless and empty of meaning if they stand

as enemies over against the eternal ideal. They never succeed in their final intent and never can. The moral nature
of man in the large always rebels against them, always casts
them out and reapplies itself after each interruption to the
one and only task. And that task is not the avaunting of one
individual or one group of men or nation in power over
another, but the lifting up of all men together. Or as the
creative spirit puts it—the fashioning of an ever more perfect world in which all men can share. We know this
instinctively as joyful and true, and the unforgivable evil,
the unpardonable sin against this privilege and principle is
to cease to remember it, is to cease to struggle for it.

Such is the demand of a real democracy.

v

And so the message has run through the ages like a
musical theme in the symphony of life, or like a beacon
flashed from mountain top to succeeding mountain top.
And always the voice of the poet, the artist, the creator
has spoken the summons clearest, has held the torch farthest
aloft. Now in our own land our poets and singers, following
Whitman, here and there have caught the song, have seen
the gleam, and are adding their word to the universal
proclamation, their spark of fire to the eternal flame. And
what we need now is more poets, more than ever before—
more singers, more laborers in the vineyard of this our one
true Lord. And only when we've got them can we hope
to swell the scattered jubilate, the individual *te deum*, into
an inspiring chorus sounding again the everlasting refrain
of man's divine search for his haven and his home. Only
thus can we create here in these United States another of
the mountain peak times with their quenchless flame which
it is our privilege and duty to create.

Interpreting America

Some years ago I struck up a passing acquaintance with a contracting engineer on a train—a man of flowing words and very definite opinions. We were sitting on the rear platform of the lounge car as we rode through the mountains of Pennsylvania. He was talking about this vast country of ours and the writers in it.

"Why don't you literary folks really try to interpret America?" he said. "When I was younger I loved to read modern novels, I loved to go to the theatre, but after getting out into the world and helping build such things as these great steel bridges we've been crossing or that hydroelectric plant we passed a few minutes back, I began to lose interest in most of the printed stuff as well as what I saw on the stage. And the movies don't seem to be any better either. Of course I like to go to a movie now and then, or a light musical comedy. But they mean nothing." And he waved his hand dismissingly. "The movies are getting harder to take all the time anyway. Hollywood seems to be mainly concerned these days with stories of spies and gangsters, of killings and violence and cheap sex for its bill of fare. And the actors and actresses themselves don't behave normally any more. Take the way they make love on the screen—hardly decent in the close-ups. More of bitings and gnawings than kisses of true affection. Disgusting."

"Well—"

"And there is always this he-man fisticuffing going on and the jerking out of pistols either to drill somebody through the belly or to crack a skull. And when the movies are not doing that they're all the time chasing coveys of poor old Indians over the plains and shooting and murdering them. Now what sort of way is that to interpret America, I ask you, interpret it to your young people and our older ones too for that matter, and to the world at large? A fellow who'd traveled in Asia a lot told me recently that the Hollywood movies are doing more harm to our good relationships there than all the blunders of the politicians in Washington. There are exceptions now and then of course—as in the work of Charlie Chaplin and Walt Disney. And sometimes there's a healthy piece like the ones Will Rogers used to do. But as I say, they are all exceptions. Wonder to me the whole country's not filled with juvenile delinquents, and from what I read in the papers sometimes I think it is.

"Take this train we are riding on, for instance," he continued. "Here's one of the marvels of power and efficiency in the modern world. And those bridges I mentioned and the tunnels and the great skyscrapers and the stretching highways—the wide fields and farms, the harvests of grain and corn in the Middle West, the tremendous irrigation projects in the Southwest, the Roosevelt and Hoover dams —think of them. What an inspiring thing the Empire State Building is too! And Rockefeller Center! My business is as a builder—the making of such things—and yet I never get used to the wonder of them. The other day I was standing in Radio City. I looked up the corner of a structure shouldering its way some nine hundred feet in the air, its top hidden in the foggy clouds. Lord, it looked like it would lean over and crush me. Made me feel like taking off my hat and being humble before it and singing praises to the men who made it. And there I could put my hand on the jointure of the mortar and stone and steel, the true straight mark of the trowel on the cement of the unknown builder who had helped raise this mighty thing."

"Maybe you ought to write—write plays and books yourself," I said.

"Oh no, not me."

"You've got the words all right."

"I don't know about that, but I do know that most of the modern books I've read and the plays I've seen on the stage and screen seem mighty poor stuff compared to the actual things I've experienced—no lift to them, no spring and no bounce. And, brother, take it from me, this country's got plenty of lift, plenty of bounce."

"That's right," I said. "I wish it were different—our interpretations, I mean."

"And it could be different," he went on, "if the fellows that write and paint and compose our music and do what they call dabble in the arts knew and felt what this country is. Most of them stay shut up in a room or congregate around Times Square, or hang about at Hollywood cocktail parties where everybody's messing with somebody else's wife. And they don't know anything. They are ignorant, that's what."

"But a few of our writers have done some mighty fine things."

"Maybe so—away back yonder, no doubt—fellows like Emerson, Longfellow, Hawthorne, Whitman and Mark Twain. 'Course I could never get fired up over that Hawthorne—he was always too slow. I'll never forget how bored I was with that *House of Seven Gables* I had to read in high school. But still I got something from it—something about man and his duty, about what a fellow ought to do and feel in his heart—about his duty to God even, about right and wrong. But you don't hear much about duty and responsibility any more. Nor about sin, that good old word we used to use. Such words have all gone out of fashion in favor of psychiatry and sick souls—though they don't use the word soul any more, except in the church, and nobody pays much attention to the preachers. Recently I tried to read a piece—rather my wife read it to me—full of rats and death and bones and dying again—some sort of title about the Wasteland. Couldn't make a thing out of it."

" 'The rattle of the bones and chuckles spread from ear to ear—a rat crept softly through the vegetation—dragging his slimy belly on the bank—a current undersea picked his bones in whispers.' "

"Is that from the poem?"

"Yes."

"You know it by heart?"

"Some of it."

"You might have spent your time better learning something else."

"Like what?"

"Well—like the one me and my wife learned together once—'Grow old along with me, the best is yet to be.' "

"*Rabbi Ben Ezra.* I once learned it too—used to recite it to myself."

"And then it goes on to say something about 'the last of life for which the first was made.' "

"Yes, Browning was a great optimist," I said.

"Well, what's wrong with being an optimist? He had love and he had faith too. This fellow of the Wasteland was all the time discouraged. As I say, I didn't understand what he was writing about, but I got enough of it to see that he didn't think being born into this world was worth a hoot. I happen to think it is."

"So do I. But then T. S. Eliot is interpreting his age."

"What age? Not mine, anyhow. And it's not only the writing fellows and the poets and the motion picture guys and the playwrights. It's our musicians too—I mentioned them. They swing around, jazz up their stuff, pour out ungodly discords, bang on their drums and tin pans, act important like all get-out, same as if they were offering up Beethoven or Brahms. And it's all sound and fury."

"You're really down on things," I said.

"Danged tooting, such things as these," he said. "Take this modern art—it's just as bad off as any of it. I've seen some of it in the exhibition halls and museums—smeary daubs and weird wild things like what a child might make in a tantrum with paint on its fingers—the sort of thing you'd expect from people in asylums maybe with their moonlit eyes. Yes sir, I like the good old paintings, the good portraits and landscapes, things you can look at and understand—religious paintings like Raphael and Rembrandt and landscapes like Winslow Homer. And then in sculpture— fellows like Augustus Saint-Gaudens. Did you ever see that thing he did in Rock Creek Cemetery there in Washington?"

"Yes," I said, "the monument to the wife of Henry Adams. It's wonderful."

"Wonderful is right," he answered. "A figure of black grief it is. But you notice her chin is lifted, her head unbowed no matter what suffering and sorrow she has been through. There's no whining and complaining in her. She is saying her say, singing her song right on to the end. Yes."

"Well, how would you go about getting the kind of writing and the music and painting you describe?" I queried.

"Lord, I don't know," he said, throwing away the stub of his cigar and rising. "That's up to all you fellows."

He started back into the train, then turned and sat energetically down again. "Yes, I do know how," he said. "Let the authors and artists and composers get down and study and learn what this country is about just the way we engineers and builders have to study and learn what we are dealing with. And if they did that they'd appreciate it, they'd be inspired by it, yes-siree. They couldn't help it. Instead of so many of 'em sitting around and trying to read wisdom into their umbilical buttons or pour out the plaints of their sick and feeble souls, let them lift up their heads and look out before them, look out and around and back down the long reach of our history, say. We've had plenty of great things happening in this country. And great people too. Why don't they write about them for a change?

"Last winter my wife and I decided we'd try the New York theatre again. So we went up to the big city to see a few plays. We had a week and we were really going to enjoy ourselves even at five, six dollars a ticket. But seemed like every play we saw had to do with some sort of human rot and decay or degradation—yes, had to do with some poor weakling or other who was sitting about moaning over the failure of his life, sitting on a sofa or gazing out through the window and sounding off his complaint that the world had gypped him. One fellow, for instance, had learned finally that all through his boyhood days he had hated his father and he hadn't known it but that was the reason he had been frustrated so long and hadn't amounted to anything. Of course you ask yourself, that now he'd found out what the trouble was, why didn't he go on and get to work and quit sitting around rehashing the whole thing. And then in other pieces there was a lot of talk about this man Freud and the darker insides of a person that carry him helpless down to hell and deep water. And of course insanity was a big subject too, all mixed in with a good sprinkling of perversion and filth and that sort of stuff. We saw two plays dealing with these subjects—no, one and a half, for we didn't sit through the last one. The young men in those two plays with their pajamas and their perfume and their quick excited gestures and high voices were really tangled up with one another's souls—or insides or whatever you call it. I don't know how the second play ended, but along toward the end of the first one, one of them sick young fellows sat down and wrote a long note of explanation to the world, then went into the bathroom and shot himself through the head. I said to myself, that's a good riddance, but I still asked myself what good did that do him or anybody else?"

"What play was that?" I asked. "I don't remember it."

"Well, maybe I exaggerated some, but that's the way I remember it."

"I see you're always looking for a play or a work of art to do you some good."

"Of course I am. A man would be a fool to go hunting for something to do him harm. Anyway, I know that what those two young fellows needed was to be run out of their apartment—an apartment maybe which their hard-working parents somewhere, maybe down there in your North Carolina, were sending them money to pay for while they got started in their careers on the stage or found themselves. Yes sir, they should have been run out of there and put back into the fields hoeing tobacco and corn or set to swinging an axe cutting cordwood back home.

"And then there was another play about a young girl who was restless and dissatisfied and got to committing sin with a lot of young bucks in the neighborhood. Now notice of course she never spoke of it as being a sin. She was restless and dissatisfied and was looking for self-fulfillment, she said. She had such a yearning! And I might say here that sometimes that's a good way for a girl to get self-fulfillment and exactly in the manner you might expect—if she's not careful. Well, she had a flood of fine pretty phrases to explain her behavior, and as I say, sinfulness was not one of them. The fellow that wrote it could really handle the words all right, but the words didn't get anywhere even after two hours, except to show her becoming more unhappy and restless all the time. Finally she got herself raped good and thorough by the hired man to see what that would do for her. But that didn't seem to help her either, and finally the doctor came and said she was crazy and they'd have to shut her up. So they hauled her off to the asylum and the curtain came down and there was loud applause, and all around me were a lot of women sniffling in their handkerchiefs and furs and scrubbing the tears out of their eyes. I felt like standing up and saying— What that woman needs is a good hard spanking on her itching behind. And she ought to be put to work scrubbing floors or waiting on tables or doing something to make an honest living—that's what I felt like saying.

"Well, I could go on and tell you more of this same sort of thing, but my wife and I had had enough and so we turned in the rest of our six-dollar tickets and took the train back home to get cleaned off. Now you tell me," he pushed on belligerently, "why our authors can't write about better things than these? Why don't they write about what I was talking of a while ago? Write about the men who made this country, for instance—who really went up against things, men who fought their way on through and won—though plenty of them lost their lives in the struggle —the fellows that first started this country. They were men—they had a man's job to do. Yes sir, their story was a story of hardship, of flesh against stone, of steel against wood, of sweat, of heartache, of backache and all the pains and troubles of striving men conquering this great wilderness here. And they got defeated again and again. But finally they had won their precarious and shaky foothold on the fringes of this eastern shore of America. Then they beat their way inland up into the hills, into the mountains, over the mountains—mountains that I've helped tunnel through—across the rivers and plains to still other mountains and another ocean three thousand miles away. They were tough men and they were men with a vision too, with their eyes lifted, their foreheads up in the light. They are worth writing about. And then the men that followed these first pioneers! Why don't the fellows write about George Washington, for instance—about Jefferson, Franklin, Madison, Patrick Henry and Hamilton and the great work they did? And then there was Abraham Lincoln too and Teddy Roosevelt and more lately Woodrow Wilson. Now Woodrow Wilson tried one of the hardest jobs any man ever tackled—he tried to get the nations of the world to live in peace and stop cutting one another's throats all the time the way they've been doing throughout history. He's a big subject for any writer, any artist, any composer. And then we've got a lot of folklore and legends, folk tales, folk heroes and ballads to write about and use—such fellows as Davy Crockett and Paul Bunyan and the muscle man John Henry that hammered in the mountain till his hammer caught on fire. And then our inventors and our builders—Eli Whitney, Robert Fulton and the greatest of them all, Thomas A. Edison. Here is plenty of material, plenty of subject matter to last these authors a long time if they'd only see it."

"But you wouldn't want to limit writers and composers, would you—prescribe what they should write about? You wouldn't want them to write about America all the time?"

"Of course I wouldn't. But what I'm saying is they're

neglecting the very best subjects of all and choosing, it seems to me, about the worst. And why should people want to celebrate and concern themselves all the time with sicknesses and weaknesses? Why not sing about, talk about, man's strength sometimes? What people need, it seems to me, is encouragement rather than discouragement. Take yourself—what do you write about?"

"Mostly Negroes and Southern white people—"

"Poor whites?"

"I guess so. Tenant farmers pretty much."

"Uhm." He grimaced and lit another cigar. "And with a lot of sex and violence in it?"

"A lot of violence anyway, I'm afraid."

"Killings and lynchings and Ku Klux and that sort of thing?"

"Yes. You see, you have to have a lot of activity, violence even, in order to have drama."

"Seems to me you could have plenty of drama in taking a worthwhile man who's got a hard job to do and seeing how he does it."

"In the main I agree with you," I said. "The truth is we writing fellows haven't measured up to our job, I guess. But recently I tried something like what you've been talking about."

"Well, good then."

"A play dealing with some of the early history of our country."

"All right, tell me about it."

"It has to do with Sir Walter Raleigh's attempts to make a settlement on Roanoke Island in North Carolina back in the sixteenth century."

"Roanoke Island? That was where Viriginia Dare was born, wasn't it, the first English child born in the new world? I studied it in my school history as a boy. That

Sir Walter Raleigh was a man that really put out. He was right in there pitching to the end."

"Yes, he was, though all his efforts ended in failure and he lost his head to boot."

"So he lost it. But he lost it in a good cause."

"His colony of men, women and children he sent over to Roanoke Island disappeared from the face of the earth. The play is about that Lost Colony. We have produced it in an amphitheatre which we built on the island right where the colony lived."

"And how did the public like your play?"

"The people seemed to like it all right. We had big crowds that came from everywhere. We plan to run it summer after summer."

"And I reckon you showed how those settlers struggled, didn't you, how they kept on trying to make a go of things, didn't you?"

"Yes I did. There was some of the moaning and belly-aching you spoke about in it. But the main characters were tough. They were fighters. They didn't quit. They wouldn't give up. They kept right on."

"That's the way to do it."

"They suffered hunger and death and cold and disease but they wouldn't call for the calf rope."

"Calf rope is good."

"Finally they marched away into the wilderness hunting a better home and were never heard of again. But in the play I tried to show that the example of their struggle, their sacrifice, their endeavor to stand up under adversity were worth remembering. Their story is part of our heritage."

"Sounds interesting. Maybe I'll get my wife and come down and see it next summer."

"I wish you would. I'm writing another one now to be

produced in an amphitheatre we're building at Williamsburg, Virginia. It's a play about Thomas Jefferson and all the hard work he put out along with George Washington, Patrick Henry and others to get our government started back in the eighteenth century."

"Sounds good. I hope you'll keep on and write more like them. I bet you they'll be successful."

"I expect to. But there are a lot of drawbacks to this kind of drama. You see, a play in the outdoors is different from one indoors. For one thing there's not much time for characterization. There's not much time to establish mood, atmosphere and environmental background. And in order to keep a big crowd interested, overcome the crying of children and the noise of the outdoors around, things have to move in a hurry. There have to be color, pageantry, a lot of crowd action, battle scenes even."

"Well, why not? That's all a part of our life. That's healthy. It's strong and human. And always the weather."

"I've invented a name for this type of play," I continued. I was now just as full of my part of the subject as he had been of his. "I call it symphonic drama."

"Do you use a symphony orchestra in it?"

"No, not a symphony. I mean that I try to use all the arts of the theatre working together, sounding together in the Greek meaning of the term symphony. The words of the story line itself of course are the main part of the play. But I add to it and intensify it as I can with other elements of theatre art—music, pantomime, dancing, folk songs and hymns when needed, dream sequences, masks, amplification, mental speech, sound-track effects, mechanical projection devices even—whatever is needed to drive the story on to its fulfillment. I think it is possible that this sort of historical drama may spread—if we can get one or two more plays established at important historical shrines like

Valley Forge, Plymouth Rock or Gettysburg. And later these dramas won't have to be limited to historical subjects alone. Any subject matter out of the life of our people will be good if it is dramatic, at least I think it will. Our tradition is rich and varied. We are a nation of boundless enthusiasm and good health, of muscle power and the out-doors—just as you say. Our hearts and bodies are full of singing and dancing and poetry too, plenty of it. We can use all that in these plays. Yes sir, as a people our faces are lifted, our hands are eager and our feet are marching on. The outpourings of our American life are too rich and creative to find complete dramatic expression in the narrow and killingly expensive confines of any professional theatre, be it on Broadway or in any other metropolitan center. I agree with you in that. But as I say—"

"No buts, brother, you're talking my language."

"Well, I hope the Williamsburg play I am writing will be as much a success as *The Lost Colony*—yes, more so. If it is I'll feel that something of my point is proved—your point, too."

"Right."

"For every nation, it seems to me," I hurried on, "is en-gaged in the process of building a civilization or not. And just as with Greece, no nation is any greater than the heroes it honors and believes in. So I guess in this symphonic out-door drama I am engaged in the business of trying to help establish worthwhile heroes."

"And it's worthwhile work," he affirmed heartily.

"I call this play I'm working on now *The Common Glory*."

"Sounds like a good title."

"I got it from a speech made by that fiery old radical, Sam Adams, up in Boston back in Revolutionary times. To me it means there is a common glory in our American way of life, to be earned and shared by all of us, high and low, as we work to make our democratic ideal prevail. I try to show that in the play. Then another outdoor drama I want to write has to do with the first permanent settlement at Jamestown in Virginia. There were some great and heroic doings on that little island back in the early sixteen-hundreds."

"Yeah, there were that. I remember the Starving Time from my school books. And Pocahontas and John Smith."

"And John Rolfe, don't forget him—the fellow that taught the doctrine of hard work with your hands, growing things out of the earth. He believed that was the way to build a nation."

"Yeh, I remember him and his tobacco."

"But as I say, there are a lot of drawbacks to this sort of drama. There are a lot of difficulties, problems to be solved, and I haven't yet solved them."

"Well, what of it? A difficulty, a problem is a kind of opportunity, I should say. It is in my work."

"No doubt it is. But I don't agree with all you say about Broadway, bad as it is. Some mighty fine things have been done and are being done there—by Eugene O'Neill, Maxwell Anderson, Robert Sherwood and others. And I want to keep on writing for the Broadway theatre too."

"Well, suit yourself. But I like this symphonic thing you talk about. And if you believe in it, stick to it, you'll lick the drawbacks and difficulties you find in it. That's our American way—to lick difficulties. And the people will support you in it. Watch my words and see if they don't."

"I hope so."

"They will. Look beyond that curve yonder, will you—that bridge we're coming to! What a thing! Swinging right out in space across that river—a thousand feet of suspension from pier to pier. Man, man! Beautiful!"

"It is."

"Just think of it while we roll across it," he said. "Think of it—of all the sweat and hard labor that went into its making."

"I'm thinking," I said.

The Theatre and the Screen

One day when I was a little boy I stood with my father in a side show at the state fair and saw a miracle happen on a screen. A tiny puppet man in a top hat was shown diving from a high platform into a swimming pool and then springing backward out of the water and up onto his perch again. The tent that day was crowded with farmers and their wives and children who had come to see the sword swallower and the wild man from Borneo. But when for the last act this jerky little figure came walking along the side of the tent as it were, made his manikin bow to us the audience, and then went twirling down from his high perch into the water, and zoop! back again up the way he'd come, we thought no more of smoking knives or bloody meat that day. Later at night the farmers, their wives and children, all on the roads that led home like lengthening spokes from the bright city to the rim of darkness, were talking of this wonder.

"But the thing moved like a real man, Mommee."

"So it did move. It was a man."

"How did they make it move like that?"

"You tell him, George."

"How did they, Poppee?"

"Edison and such fellows can do anything these days."

"But he dived somersaults backwards and up in the air, I bet twenty feet."

"Them fellows are smart, I tell you."

"But Poppee— A man can't really do that, can he, Poppee?"

"Go to sleep, son, I tell you."

II

In 1915 *The Birth of a Nation* came to our capital city. The newspapers and wayside signs worked up a lot of interest in our section, and I rode off to see it. After a trip of several hours over thirty-five miles of miry road in a T-model Ford, I arrived at the crowded theatre door and finally made my way inside and up into the balcony. Every seat in the house was taken. The lights went down, the orchestra began to play, and things started to happen. It would be hard to describe the effect of the picture on that audience. There on the screen in front of our eyes not more than twenty yards away, we saw brave armies fighting as only brave ones can. We heard the roar of cannon, the neighing of horses, saw the bleeding and the dying, the fluttering flags and banners. And all the while the thunder and beat of the orchestra whipped our souls along in the story. Now like a breath the tumult is gone, the rumble and cannonading die out, and a beautiful woodland vision entrances us. There stands the handsome Little Colonel and his exquisite Southern sweetheart, dove in hand and all, saying a fond farewell, and the music of the violin proclaims the piteousness of their love. Then with a flick the scene has changed again, and we see the dark and sliding figure of the villain prowling around a vine-clad cottage, and the evil of his nature is intensified for us in the croompy notes of the bassoons.

So the story went on unfolding, in dumb show, captions and musical sound, telling the hopes, the loves, and the dangers that beset these our heroic characters. The audience sat one moment in breathless anxiety, another moment it was applauding the short triumph of virtue and honor. And when at last the robed and wind-blown figure of the Klansman on his horse stood in a medium close-up on a hill, and the bugle in the orchestra announced with its high note that a stern and powerful force of righteousness was risen to defend the innocent ones from all villains of whatsoever creed or color, a frenzy ran among the spectators like fire among wintry broomstraw. There were yells and shouts, clenching of fists, and loud unashamed oaths. One woman directly in front of me sprang up as in a holy-roller hysteria and screamed, "Kill 'em, Kill 'em!" and then like a lady in a play or protracted meeting fell with a fainting thud to the floor. The ushers hurried up and carried her out, but even as they went, she opened her eyes and looked longingly and avidly back towards the screen. (Not until years later did I realize that without the bugle note the lady would not have fainted. It was then I understood the place of music in the theatre.)

I saw *The Birth of a Nation* many times, and its effect on the audience was always much the same. True, these audiences were Southern, and this would account for some of the emotional outbursts on racial matters, but from general reports this film was a great success in all parts of the world. (I should like to mention here that, of all the modern stage plays I have witnessed or heard about, none of them seem to have affected the audience to the degree that this melodramatic and romantic story did.)

The next event in the movies for me was Charlie Chaplin. One day in 1919 his *Shoulder Arms* was shown in a French cantonment for us American soldiers. Here again the audience was moved to vent its loud appreciation. Chuckles and gales of laughter swept through the hall at the antics of the little man, and for a while the memory of air raids, whining 75's, snipers, stink and filth of trenches was forgotten. He was the divine magician playing with the bauble of our souls for an hour. And some weeks later, when I saw the likeness of Charlot hauled through the streets of Paris and followed by a great crowd of hurrahing boys and girls, I joined in the procession which led to a moving-picture entrance. And from that day to this I have followed wherever he leads—except in politics. A few years ago I sat with a friend who, like me, was seeing *The Gold Rush* for the tenth time. After the show we spoke in guilty defense of Shakespeare and the drama and felt sad that neither of us would wish to see one of those plays ten times. But the afterthought that we had read some of Shakespeare's plays more than ten times and would continue to read them comforted us where thoughts of the stage could not.

III

Some time ago I had the chance to do some movie writing in Hollywood. With all the glaring evidence of cheap pictures that fill the world before me, and with plenty of warnings against Babylon and all its waste and iniquities, I landed at one of the major studios. This at last was the glittering world of Pirandellian make-believe, where everything seems what it is not and yet is what it seems. Here were hundreds of acres of buildings where dreams were manufactured, where thousands of people went in and out early and late creating millions of feet of film on which were imprinted little shadows which, placed against a steady light, acted, talked, and danced and spun their thousand-and-one tales of ambition, love, hope, or despair.

The first thing to do was to see inside and get acquainted with the goings-on. And so I did and tried to understand what I saw. I read all the books on the movies I could get— both European and American. I poked about in the cutting rooms, the wardrobes, the projection rooms and construction departments. I read the engineers' handbooks on light and sound devices. I made myself familiar with all the camera terms from "angle-shot" to "wipe-off." And the more I learned the more enthusiastic I became. Here indeed was the creation of the machine age which was the equal of the Word as spoken by men of old. Here was a medium infinite and universal in its power, able to depict anything—whether in heaven, or earth, or in hell; whether of man's relation to man or man's deepest submerged self. For the first time in history a completely democratic art form was available, capable of answering any vital demand made upon it by the imagination of any human being. For the first time in the history of the world we had a dramatic medium in the movies which could be understood by black and white, yellow or red, the only requirement being that the audience must be able to see or hear—better if it could do both. For pantomime is and can be understood by all men of whatever race, creed, or calling, and music likewise. A Japanese will laugh at Charlie Chaplin even as a New Yorker will.

For several weeks I labored on a script, trying to measure up in some degree to the camera which was to express the story I had to tell. No one hurried me, nobody said do this or that. Apparently I was left free to do as I chose. What was this nonsense I had heard about the cramping power of Hollywood and its slave-driving methods with writers? I began to doubt tales of woe which brethren of my kind had been wont to tell. At last my script was in some sort of final shape, and conferences with producer, director, leading actor, and men of the technical staff began. The scenario was read, discussed, and tentatively accepted. I was pleased to find that the boss men said only a little revision was needed here and there and the thing would be ready for shooting. The revisions suggested seemed sensible enough, and I gladly tried to make them. So the script was finally delivered into the producer's hands, and I began another writing job while it was being shot. Now and then, I would hear a report from the lot that "everything is going fine," and I was beginning to feel some pride in the fact that this picture was to be a little better maybe than the general Hollywood product. A few times I went on the set and watched the making and came away with nothing but admiration for the studio and its employees. How hard and seriously everybody seemed to be working—from early morning till late at night they labored. And as time went on I learned that, contrary to general report, hard work was the rule in Hollywood. Nervous breakdowns there are not all liquor, love and libidos.

When the picture was finally completed, I went downtown to see it. It turned out to be a straightforward, level, and unimpressive thing. Whatever touch of inspiration I thought I had in writing it was gone. On referring to my script, I found a bit here, a bit there, this end of a scene, this key line of a scene changed or left out. Somebody had been there while I was gone. I discussed the matter some days later with another writer—a man who formerly had been a pretty well known but struggling novelist and now was an ace scenario writer with a purple Cadillac and a seaplane to his credit. "Yes," he said, "they gave your script to me to look over. I hope you didn't mind. We often have to do that."

"Do what?" I asked.

"Well, smooth things up. You see, your script leaned too much toward one of these cussed artistic productions, and that's a thing no studio will allow. There's not a cent of money in them."

"How do you know there's not?"

"Listen, this is a business out here, not an art. You'd better go back to Greenwich Village or South Carolina."

"North Carolina," I corrected with some heat.

"Well, wherever it is."

"But Chaplin"—I began.

"Yes, Chaplin!" he snapped.

"And Disney."

"Yes, Disney," he murmured.

IV

My friend was right, as I well found out. Making pictures in Hollywood is a business, an industry, and with its present aims and methods has to be. This simple and first fact is the source of all the trouble that befalls anyone interested in the art of the cinema, whether he be actor, writer, musician, architect, dancer, sculptor, painter, or stage designer. Since the old nickelodeon days when this novel form of mass entertainment tapped a mine of riches for any hustling Jack, Harry or Sam, money-making has been its prime aim. And this being true, it was logical that, as the different studios developed, they should follow the methods of big business and in the competitive market force a speeding up and leveling out of production that would prohibit any sort of experimentation or excursions into new creations. The only experimentation they can or will afford to be interested in is that of novelty. Let any new trick or gadget be invented which might be used to intrigue the populace through the till, and the executive will grab it in an instant. But let an Eisenstein or Clair try to interest them in cinematic art and they politely but firmly refuse to hear. "We'd like to do fine things," they will always tell you, "but such pictures never pay. We'll show you the books."

The studios have a product to sell to the masses of the world, and in order to sell to everybody they think they must strike a common denominator of general illiteracy and bad taste. Their pictures are standardized by what they consider to be the intelligence quotient of the majority of people in the small villages and crossroad places. For there are many times more 14-year-old minds in the world than 30-year-old minds—and a dime is a dime no matter whose it is, and the best picture from the Hollywood point of view is the picture that attracts the most dimes. This is obvious and well known to everybody, but I mention it in order to somewhat explain, for instance, that pernicious institution known as censorship. That powerful organization is in actuality an economics-inspired liaison medium between the studios and the public. Outwardly—and hypocritically—it has as its intent the welfare of the country's morals. But what the organization really does is to keep the studios informed as to the varying whims of the 14-year-old mind and what is likely to go best in Ohio and not to go in North Carolina or vice versa.

By censoring each script carefully before shooting and reporting its findings to its employer (the producer), the censorship board saves the studios hundreds of thousands of dollars a year in wasted footage. No wonder the producers are willing to provide the salaries of that body, for after all it is one of the best paying parts of their business. And so it is that the writer who strives to create a script which in some way shall express the drama of his characters, or the problems of life as he feels them, is again and again defeated in his purpose by the censor. And once the censor says nay to a line or a scene, the writer is helpless. The producer simply has to point to the ruling of that office, if he cares

to, and say, "Here's the public board on morality and cus-
toms. It says no"—and no it is. Sometimes a producer will
overrule the censor, as in the case of a recent sensational
convict picture, but these differences of judgment are rare.

Such difficulties as these, to repeat, make it impossible for
one interested in the moving pictures as an art to sink himself in Hollywood without some total loss in time, energy,
and life's enthusiasm. He can replenish his purse perhaps,
but it is likely to prove a costly gain otherwise. There is
hardly any place on the globe so full of unhappy would-be
artists—writers, musicians, actors, and poets. They are sur-
feited with hush money, but many of them cannot hush
the gnawing that wakes them up at night when they think
of the book they had planned to write, the play they yet
will write, or the symphony that struggles somewhere
within them. They are wearied to distraction trying to provide cheap stuff at the behest of their cynical-minded and
ignorant employers, the producers—men who seem to have
a special genius for exploiting the gullibility, the appetites
and weaknesses of the public. And why should they not be
wearied, yes, wearied and undone? For what joy, what
encouragement and inspiration can there be in continuing
to assist at the corruption and pollution of a people's soul?

v

But even so, Hollywood is essentially no worse than the
old Broadway theatre, or for that matter the professional
entertainment theatre in any great metropolis, a generation
or so ago. In fact it is the old theatre in a new form. The
movies through the universality of their medium have been
able to provide more entertainment to more people at less
cost than the old professional theatre could, and the Er-
langers and Shuberts have pretty much disappeared. And

just as the art or imaginative theatre grew out of a revolt against the professional theatre, so will, I hope and think, the art of imaginative cinema grow out of the professional movies. The hundreds of dissatisfied creative minds, whose sole job day after day is the making of money for bankers, millionaires, and stockholders, will some day—and very soon at that—break into open revolt. There is no price large enough to keep a rebellious spirit indefinitely enslaved. Already a few independent producers, writers, and artists are trying a few forlorn experiments in creating pure forms of cinematic art, both here and abroad. And just as the imaginative theatre has had its Appia, its Stanislavsky, and its Craig, so will the new imaginative cinema have its apostles and philosophers who, following the lead of Charlie Chaplin and Disney, will give to the art a statement of new form and vital method. And when this new art has broken itself loose from the industry and professionalism of Hollywood and started on its own path, we shall see moving picture dramas worthy of the name. Writers, actors, directors, and musicians will then take joy and pride in their work and will strive to the best of their minds and souls to deal with the camera as its essential nature provides. And what they create will be of their own making, and the writers will be free to write scenarios as full of imagination and poetry as their gifts will allow. And these scenarios will have the dignity of publication, just as the stage plays are now published, and the author will have every privilege in the art motion picture that his brother playwright has in the art theatre.

VI

In the imaginative motion picture art, as I like to call it, which is soon to be a power in the world, this truth will be recognized; namely, that the art of screen is not the art of the theatre. And conversely the theatre—(that is, the imaginative theatre, for no other is really left, now that the movies have taken over the professional theatre)—this theatre must realize that its art is not that of the motion picture. Each has a nature of its own technique. But in each the poet as creator and story-teller shall be supreme. In the motion picture he has a means of universal and infinite power—the camera. In the theatre he likewise has a means of universal and infinite richness—the intimate presence. In the former he has an invention which eradicates all the material difficulties of depiction which beset the stage, but which projects forth only shadows of two dimensions and begins with a certain aloofness therefor. In the latter he has the embodied being which projects only itself and in three dimensions and begins with a complete and vital closeness therefor. And as the essential nature of the camera is expressed in pantomime and accompanying sound, so the essential nature of the intimate presence is expressed in words and accompanying pantomime.

Now those who lament the death of the theatre before the onslaught of the movies do not grasp the vital differences of the two mediums and likewise forget the godlike power which resides in the word spoken by the intimate presence. It is immortal and cannot die, and a theatre founded on it will never perish. The theatre is not dead. Only the worst of it is dead or moved elsewhere. Let that worst go with its methods of industry and mass marketing. The best, more purified and certain of itself shall stand, for the very purpose of time and the nature of man are that before history is finished the best shall somehow come forth to light.

But this theatre of the imaginative word and intimate presence must refit itself more in terms of the machine age if it is to be free and powerful as it should be. It must take a lesson from the flexibility and universality of the camera medium and make more flexible and universal its own medium. It must throw away the bothersome clogs of too many material props which impede the flow and lift of the dramatist's story. Slight suggestions and symbols should be sufficient. Let the poet follow his story wherever it leads— into bogs, boudoirs, or skyscrapers. Let the word speak. With the great advance in discoveries concerning light, almost any change of scenery and scene effect can be worked instantaneously; and when the curtain goes up on the stage the processes of fade-ins, fade-outs, and dissolves which the movies have discovered can be used so that the dramatist's imagination and the audience's attention remain one.

And under such conditions poetry will return again to the stage, and the freedom that Shakespeare knew in his Elizabethan theatre will be ours to enchantment. And whereas the new motion picture art form will be the imaginative sight and sound unlimited, so the new theatre will be the home of the imaginative word and vitalized being unbound. And once more, as in the days of Shakespeare, we shall be able to parade before our vision all the manifestations of nature and the subleties of the mind which are usable in the movie medium. And once more music in the theatre will return to us, above which the high poet's words are calling.

Man and His Universe

What of the universe? What do I believe about it? What does it mean to me? I ask myself these things and piteously try to answer them.

I believe in it as uncreated, everlasting, without beginning or end—uncreated insofar as having a beginning, but continuously self-creative insofar as it continues to endure. I consider it as the totality of matter or energy that is.

I believe in life which inhabits and uses this totality of matter either partially or wholly or anywhen—which was created, had a beginning in consciousness and shall have an end.

Both matter and life are forever changing—always have been, always will be (speaking of life while it exists), but the identity of their change is in name only, for matter changes helplessly, self-helplessly and blindly, and life changes for a purpose.

The fact of the creation of life, the appearance of life in this material universe was perhaps fortuitous and precedent to any purpose. But once created it was all purpose, and when it lacks purpose for long it disappears, and the matter which once contributed to it—its body—returns again to blind gurgitating energy to be used for other life and lives in other spaces and other times perchance.

This space and time we speak of are not real in themselves
—they are only words, label-concepts of description and
change. There is neither space nor time apart from matter
and life. Space applies to matter, and time applies to life.
There is no space empty of matter and no dead time except
as life is dead.

Then we have matter and living matter—or matter alive
—the inorganic and the organic in familiar terms. Our business is with the latter.

Now life seems to be of three different orders, not only
seems but is—the vegetable, the animal, and man. The animal is higher than the vegetable, and man higher than the
two.

By higher I mean of consciousness and meaningful purpose.

I said matter has no purpose and that life, once it is life,
is filled with purpose. What is that purpose? Excellence in
itself. And what is this excellence?

It is the making more and more manifest through whatever means—conscious or unconscious—whether through
thinking, feeling and doing or whatever else—the ideal
nature, the bent, intent, trend, of the living thing or animal
or person concerned.

The excellence of a tree depends on how fine a tree it is
and becomes. The excellence of an animal the same. The
excellence of a man the same.

The first two—the vegetable and the animal—have no
conscious means of working toward that end—that excellence. Therefore, they are sinless, never triumphant, never
shamed, and are beholden to no moral law. In them the
power of change is all-powerful. They are helpless in its
grip—that is, helpless in the grip of their own living organic
nature, a condition which could not be otherwise. Now
man has a conscious means of working toward his own

excellence—himself, his self, the soul. In fact the self or soul gives him his drive, his inspiration, the meaning of his life—to develop and improve himself and his world in beauty and worth about him. That is, in brief, man as a self is a spirit.

By the word spirit or spiritual I mean—in and for and by itself in terms of an idea of perfection.

Then is perfection attainable? No. The question is meaningless. For change continues, and no change in perfection would be possible except to imperfection. The nature of the perfecting process is creation and growth in and toward the ideal, and beyond perfection there could be neither. So man cannot, could not, reach perfection. But the perfecting of himself in his art, his things, his hopes, his dreams, his deeds, his loves, is his continuous privilege and duty.

Perfection lies in the struggle toward perfection. Only in this sense does the word have meaning.

II

So whether as a creature, man came into being, into existence by design or accident, whether he shall likewise disappear or not, are not his real concern. That concern is with his own living present self, his present world, and his present fellows. And in this I include responsibility to the future, of course, though not to the past, obviously. These former he can do something about. The past is beyond him except in the main as it may be memorialized.

Nor need he bother about why he is endowed with a spirit. Such a question is unreal and cannot be answered—any more than there can be a final answer to the final question about the reality (nature) of matter. The actual fact has to be accepted and business carried on from there, for the nature of first awareness is such acceptance. Suffice it then that man is a spirit and that he seek to live as a spirit.

Thus we find our time-space-change-law universe energized with these phenomena—completed in them and infused with them:

Matter
Life
Spirit

Matter is purposeless.

Life is practically purposeful and necessitous.

Spirit is ideally purposeful and free.

Between the first and the second is the mysterious linkage of consciousness, of awareness.

Between the second and the third is a man's soul, his sense of responsibility, his ethical sense, and the consciousness of free will. And this sense is incorporative of the preceding linkage of awareness. It is man's real self.

What is consciousness? The principle of awareness. It is quantitative.

What is the self? The principle of appreciation. It is qualitative.

And as the former can feed and enter into the second, so can the second become spiritual—or not.

So now begins the problem of man's ritual and curriculum toward the higher ideal of the spirit, that ideal and *art*.

Forever Growing: A Credo for Teachers

Life is like a tree forever growing, and man is in and of that life. And though he must continue to be a man as long as he exists, still he has the power to become unlike himself and ruined and beastly if he will. Nothing is protected in its *status quo ante* against the possibilities of its own future and flux and undoing, neither man's God nor fate, nor man himself. Change is forever taking place, and there is no abiding of things as they are. In any particular thing or conglomerate of things every tomorrow, every minuscule of time brings its process of differentiation and further varying. *Panta rhei*, says the weeping philosopher.

But wherefore weep?

Panta rhei, everything flows. And if the particulars, the conglomerates which make up the sum of the whole, are eternally changing, so is the universe which they constitute. Then where is permanence to be found beyond change? Where is truth with her verities to be sought for—if truth abides?

Permanence might be expected in a realm where impermanence does not appear. Naturally. We might find it in the opposite of these particulars, the whole of things perhaps. Now the opposite of things is nothings, or nothing-ness. But this is a state identical with the state of death—this opposite. Then it seems death is the permanence, the nothingness we seek. But does not death, this nothingness, also suffer change even as the particulars and conglomer-ates in life? It does.

Then there is no permanence in death. It too upboils and is activated. For life will not let it be. Life seizes upon the inert body-of-death, takes it apart piecemeal and speckmeal, plunders it, absorbs it, informs its own self with new vital-ity from it, uses it as the flame uses the wood, as the body uses the blood, as the rain the cloud, and as the sap uses the flower or the tree. But is not the wood the source of the flame, the body the source of the blood, the cloud of the rain, the flower and the tree the source of the sap, and coffined love the poet's lament? That too.

Each owes its being somewhat to the other. And insofar as one is a separate being, it is so through the vitalizing process of causation flowing in and between them. Thus in this rich and mutual altruism life goes on. The inorganic feeds the organic, and the organic is everlastingly busy growing itself into full form, reproducing its kind, either better or worse in excellence and never the same, and giving its body into death in turn for the feeding and making of its kind that comes after it. The existence of one is the perpetuity of the other.

What humility! What sacrifice! And where is the secular loose talk about the law and the red dripping tooth and claw and the survival of the fittest, meaning the most cruel!

Well, it depends upon who is seeking for what and why and how as to the findings that result. For there is in nature a basic cooperativeness and beneficence which heals and helps even as a cool spring does a panting thirst, or love does desire and food does hunger. That too. And nature's children know it. And all youthful and healthy people who have not been contaminated and corroded by the fad of analysis and dead learning and the tools and methods of pragmatic insolence, ignorance, and pride—they know it well and feel it. And this cooperativeness, this beneficence, this changing activity of need and fulfillment, of life into death and death into life is a process—the process of creation.

A wise man said, "Except a corn of wheat fall into the ground and die, it abideth alone." And he also said, "Greater love hath no man than this, that a man lay down his life for his friend." And another said, "How are the dead raised up? And with what body do they come? Thou foolish one, that which thou sowest is not quickened except it die." And still another said—a voice of antiquity, ever-vital and ever-creative and spilling out its enrichment and encouragement for man—this voice said—"And now abideth faith, hope, charity, these three; but the greatest of these is charity."

The world process is creative then, both as to particulars and as to the whole! That is the truth, that is the permanence we require.

II

But this is an old and obvious truth to us—or it should be. We have heard it from Samson and his riddle of the bees and the honey and the bones, from the weary wanderer and the riddle of the sphinx. We heard it from Plato in his metaphysic of mortality and immortality and darkness and light. Plotinus and Origen told us the same. And so did the great and learned Doctor of the thirteenth century, persuading us afresh to the freedom of the will, moral responsibility, intellectual love and the salvation of souls. And before him his own master Aristotle spoke out his intuition and seeing of the nature of virtue and the good life in a world of practical affairs.

And the same refrain was told to his love in later centuries by Petrarch, whom the scholars hold as "the first modern man" and who no doubt would have felt surprised and lonely in his century if he had known he was to be that. And before him was Dante with his epic of endurance and attainment, and before him Boethius. And later Erasmus, and the great Jew of Amsterdam, and the sickly Bacon, and much later the heavy plodding-footed Hegel and the healthful aristocratic Goethe—all said the same.

These and a thousand others like them have stood up along the path of literature and life and affirmed this truth. They have risen as living witnesses for the great process of creativeness, of life like a tree forever growing, or a mighty river forever flowing. But their words and their works have too often been in vain, most often have been in vain. We have not heard them.

III

For we teachers and scholars, caught in a scientific dispensation, find it impossible to accept life as a miracle of creativeness and growth. We are conditioned to believe that anything smacking of a miracle is perforce somehow mystic, medieval, sentimental, vaguely subjective and therefore unsound, not stopping to consider that the process of raising the question even is itself miraculous. It is the old scholasticism back again. And we fetch out our commonsense curricula and scientific methodologies and put them to bear upon the matter as if it were an object to be measured and described under a microscope.

And that's what we do—measure and describe, and set down findings. We categorize, catechize, cut up, analyze and compare and put appraisals upon the process of life, and not only upon life but upon art and literature—which is worse. In place of life and art and literature, we thus substitute a method of derivation, matters of influence and style and types—whether of classic, romantic, realistic, naturalistic, expressionistic, or what not, and on down to as many adjectival examples of labeling as we can dig out of our inkwells or typewriters, being therefore the more solid and scientific in our results, we say.

IV

And these labels we schoolmasters make and try to paste on the creative process of life are forever peeling off in the turn and twist and scouring of time. They will not stick. How could a label stick on a flowing river, or a stamp on shaking gay green leaves? But our scholastic activity continues. As soon as one label wears out or peels off or is blown away in contrary winds of doctrine, or passes out of fashion, we have another and more scientific one ready for the pasting. And much of the frustration in purposes and hindrances to man's development and joy occur because of this confusion of labels and names which we are responsible for. They are seals and deceptions stuck not so much perhaps on the body of the process of life and art itself, as over the eyes of both the seeker and the seer.

Consider a term universally honored and respected by the schoolmen—to wit, nature's law. What confounding of wisdom and experience occurs in its name! A law of nature! The law! How it closes up the eyes of those who would look directly at the wonder and glory of the moon or the stars themselves, but cannot see the object for the law which has it in thrall and makes it behave according to its will, the thing itself having no will. But there is in actual fact no law in nature, neither in the world of trees and men and growing things nor in the wheeling cindered stars. What we call the law is the way things act.

But this sort of learning and mathematical formularizing are understandable and necessary in the world of things— science. Through them we are "able to do business" with our environment. Through them the multitudinous phenomena of life around us are sifted out, catalogued, schematized and made amenable to the immediacy of our practical standards and needs. Thus science. But literature, art, life, are not sciences, not scientific. Still we keep on trying to deal with them as sciences, as "things" even.

Natural law, then, is but a label or word-concept which we apply to change. It is a product of man's mind, an attribute he has given, a reading he has taken and made fast in the books. Things change. In order to change they have to change the way they do change or they could not change. Since they change the way they do change, we say they change according to the law of change, a causal sequence in time and space, and these last two are more labels or word-concepts. The truth is they simply change. It is their nature to change, their creative nature. And rather than being beholden to any law, the law as we describe it is beholden to them. They create the law, self-create it. And potentially at any instant of "time" and any point in "space" an object may behave in a new creative way, a way it has never behaved before. It may even turn into its opposite nothing, or a nothing may suddenly become a thing—as is happening all the time. The process, then, varies in itself but it cannot behave "unlawfully," that is, contrary to itself.

This is the essential mystery of the universe which consciousness perceives and can wonder at and worship, but which its understanding cannot penetrate and should not.

For to do so consciousness would have to become other than itself, other than the process, which it can never do. Consciousness, awareness—which is identical with the process—cannot be conscious of its own cessation. And if the cessation of consciousness has ever been witnessed it has never known that fact, and the witness himself became the embodiment of that which was witnessed—as is well told in many books of the orient.

And between this awareness, this conscious mind, and the creative vital world, we educators and professors place these misleading signs and tokens and distortions of meaning. And in doing so we are betraying our trust both as persons and as teachers; we betray our experience and its meaning for the future.

We are back at the old business of practicing the heresies of abstract medieval authority, except in this case the evil of abstraction is intensified. For we have made it of a lower scientific down-gazing earthly order, whereas in the old days of the wandering friar and hungry scurvy-bitten monk the gaze, however blinded, was upward and into a beneficent heaven.

v

We scholars and teachers are tough-hided sinners, though, and good party members all right. We will do anything in the name of our creed or cause. We are propagandists of the veriest sort, and the hapless quivering body of truth is inquisitioned, quartered and drawn on any class or feast day. Look at the books we put out, the articles we print, our swarming midges of marginal footnotes, our journals, catalogues, compendia, our editions of volumes of art and volumes of literature, our floods of anthologies. And where is wisdom among them!

Everywhere we cut up life and the green creations of life into just such categories, movements, influences, currents, schools and the like, as mentioned above. And at any time we wish, we will reach and take a living artist, or a dead one, lift him from the fireside or dell of his creative activity, place him on the shelf and catalogue him. And any student or seeker for wisdom and joy from this artist may come as if to a dead idol in a temple. But shining big for him to see first of all is a huge label or card or notice which proclaims this artist as of such and such a type—not just an artist, but a certain kind of artist. And the emphasis is always on the kind and not the art itself. And the pity is that, nearly every time, the label or card or notice gives life the lie. As time well proves. But the confused young neophyte does not find that out for many years after, maybe never. And he stays away from the temple.

And as with artists, so we do with other living souls whether they be preachers, politicians, or philosophers.

In a large and popular anthology of world literature now lying before me I notice that Zola and Maupassant have been labeled in heavy letters as being in the category of the Naturalistic School—whatever that means. Apparently the editor is following along in dog-leash obedience with hundreds of other editors who have preceded him and uses several pages of ad hoc writing showing what is meant by naturalism and proving beyond a doubt and without rebuttal that these two authors, along with such others as Gorki and Dreiser, are condemned to this classification till the lake of Belial freezes over and there's nothing to be done about it. Only as exponents and representatives, propagandists and exemplifiers of naturalism shall we know them.

I turn a wad of pages back in the same anthology and find that Aeschylus and Sophocles are representative of the classical period or school or age and nothing else. And from the editor's long and thorough essay on the nature of classicism, its balance and restraint, I am persuaded what vastly different creatures these four men were. In fact they were not four men. They were four propagandists—two for naturalism, two for classicism. And so it goes.

What a confusion of tongues we editors and scholars indulge in! Ah, these labels! Are there not blood and thunder and guts and organs of fecundity, liver and lights, tumors, thighs, stallions, procreation and abundant animal life in the stately "classical" drama and in Homer's epics even as in the "naturalistic" Zola and Maupassant! Yes, plenty of them, plenty of "naturalism." In fact Aeschylus out-Zolas Zola. Open up the *Agamemnon* and read the scene where the wild and turbulent Cassandra sees the children of Thyestes sitting as gory phantoms above the doomed king's house. "See ye these infants sitting here on the palace like to phantoms of dreams?—Children just as if they had perished by the hands of their kinsmen—their hands crammed with the meat of their own entrails, a piteous mess, of which their father tasted."

Or take another of his plays, *The Eumenides*, and read the scene, for instance, in the interior of the temple of Apollo where we can see and hear the shuddering and grotesque and wild snaky-headed women, hear their whimpering moanings, their scaly raspy movements and see rising from the ground the ghost of murderous and murdered Clytemnestra smoking with her own blood. Or turn to the golden and symmetrical, classic Sophocles and read how Oedipus tears out his own eyes, after having killed his own father and married his own mother and begot four children, half-brothers and sisters to himself. And there, see, the tragic queen Jocasta hanging from a rafter by the neck dead of shame and grief!

And consider sad and mellow Euripides with all his murders and betrayals and gods in the machine, and the story of his hysterical bloody Medea, mother and killer of children, her own. And pick up Homer again and read of his devastations and lust and blood, the spearing and letting out of brains, the defilement of Hector's body, the eating of the dead by dogs, the hate and treachery and cunning, the quarrels among the gods, the bickering of Aphrodite and Athena, and the god of war himself running with cowardly howls over the plain, and then the crafty double-dealing Odysseus. And so on, and so on.

Yes, here are fervency and excess—both as to content and form!

VI

When we forget our tokens and labels and signs and hierarchy of pigeon-holing and think of the works, the stories and plays and poems themselves, we find that they are part of the creative process of life and men in life, and as such we can enjoy them, draw from them, be enriched and refreshed through them. Our learned findings of influences and kinds and types only get in the way and are a hindrance. They get between the appreciator and the object of his appreciation—that is, a really *felt* appreciation. And they are deadly for the creative artist. In fact a creative artist can learn only from a preceding work or art or master if he thinks of the painting as painting and the painter or poet as a creative, kindred soul, a fellow technician working at a job, never giving a hang as to what school or movement he might belong to. And what is true of the creative apprentice is just as true if not truer of the student and critic. And if it is true of these why is it not also true for us teachers and schoolmen?

For do we not all live by the same bread of life!

Even as I write out these words my daughter is down-stairs doing a paper for her scholarly professor on "Cole-ridge as Romanticist." What of Coleridge as just—poet? Or what of Coleridge's poetry—just that—with all its magic and music and exquisite imagination and delicacy of tone and touch and thought? Why not have her write about them? And why ever any such label as "Romanticist" to bring her nearer to him when it puts him farther off? Why not just let him be, and let all the others be, and so let her receive them and their fire and glory and delight into her young soul? These should be the matter of interest, of con-cern and inspiration.

But instead she has to be, at the hard and blind and bull-headed behest of her professor, searching her young noggin for secondhand and unfelt words that will show she has surprised the secret out of the sage of Hampstead, and henceforth will know the old, loquacious, metaphysical boy for what he is—not a spirit and a miraculous soul but a type, an example of a movement writ down by us school-men as romanticism. It may take her years to recover from this damage and wrong-filling of her mind, this wrong-teaching which dries up her emotions and dissipates her dreams. She may get contaminated by this jargon of analyz-ing and "sciencizing" and go out as a teacher of literature herself and help contaminate others. She may never be able to approach Coleridge again, fresh and unprejudiced and pure as she should—approach him with an open heart in which the seeds and images of his beauty may thrillingly fall and as thrillingly grow. And so she will move on to the next poet who stands in line as a representative of the move-ment, Wordsworth, and make the same tragic failure of missing the fragrance and breath of his quickened work, fail completely to feel the creative wonder of what he wrote, setting him down in emptiness the while—Romanticist.

VII

I remember one lonely Sunday on the farm when I was a boy. The day before in town I had met up with a book-peddler and bought a copy of Shakespeare's *Hamlet* for a quarter. And with the family gone off to church and the house silent and empty, I read the play. And as I read, I grew more interested and filled with suspense as to the people and their fate in the drama. And emotion became more and more packed up in me. And finally I came to the scene where poor piteous Ophelia enters with brains broken and mind deranged, speaking her little mad and anguished sayings—"there's rue for you, and here's some for me. We may call it herb of grace o' Sundays. O, you must wear your rue with a difference. There's a daisy. I would give you some violets, but they withered all when my father died. They say he made a good end." (Singing.) "For bonny sweet Robin is all my joy." And the tears gushed from my eyes, my heart opened with a yearning deep and wide—

> "O wert thou in the cauld blast,
>   On yonder lea, on yonder lea,
>   My plaidie to the angry airt,
>   I'd shelter thee, I'd shelter thee."

That day was a mark in my life. And because of that fresh, wild appreciation, untrammeled and unprepared for by any professorial coaching as to influences and types and methods by which the play might have been derived to represent the Elizabethan age or something other than itself—because of that, *Hamlet* has stood solidly by me, a rich storehouse to draw from again and again through the years and has meant more to me than it otherwise could possibly have meant. And Ophelia has continued to live her sweet and piteous life in the recesses of my soul.

Another lonely hot Sunday on the farm, I was lying in my sweaty little shed room reading the Bible, when I came upon the twelfth chapter of *Ecclesiastes*. I suddenly sat up in delight at what I read—the beauty of it thrilled me and put a stuffiness in my throat. I hurried out of the room and down the side porch into the kitchen where my sister was getting lunch. "Listen, Mary," I said, "listen." And I read, " 'Or ever the silver cord be loosed, or the golden bowl be broken, or the pitcher be broken at the fountain or the wheel broken at the cistern.' "

"That's wonderful," she said. And she stood by the stove, holding a little piece of firewood balanced in her hand, her eyes wide and thoughtful as she went on hearing the words over a second time in her mind. "Read it again," she said. And I did, and for a while we shared the beauty and wonder of those lines and others in the chapter. And because of that experience, *Ecclesiastes* has always remained one of my favorite books. I thank my stars that I was not "prepared" for it by the usual teacher, say, of Comparative Literature, who talked of a preceding Stoic philosophy and currents of Hebraic pessimism which brought the book to being—a resultant of clearly demarked and discernible scholarly laws and forces. For it would have been marred before I got to it—as so many of the great works of literature were marred for me in precisely that way.

VIII

And through the blue depths of the sky the bird flies, but the tips of its wings are never stained in it. Moreover it is written—that with faith a man thinks. Faithless he cannot think. And he who worships God as the great King milks heaven and drinks it day by day. His food is never exhausted. . . . "And he shall be like a tree planted by the rivers of water, that bringeth forth his fruit in his season; his leaf also shall not wither, and whatsoever he doeth shall prosper."

For life is like a tree forever growing!

Love, Hate and Tragedy

I

The two primary guides of the self—and by primary I mean first and instinctive—through life are evidently pleasure and pain—or joy and sorrow, happiness and misery, gladness and sadness, and so on. And just as the self or soul cannot be analyzed further, so pleasure and pain cannot be further analyzed, even though they may be described and causally derived by logic. For they precede any process or method of analysis at any moment. And all such analysis is obviated in the very nature of the act of experiencing, of feeling.

Then it follows that we by nature like what pleases us and dislike what pains us. On the one hand we wish to take in, to absorb, to embrace, to have more of. And on the other hand we wish to push away, to repel, to avoid, and to have less of.

On the one hand we love, and on the other we hate.

Now love works for unity and identity among all selves or souls. Hate works for disunity and disparity of all selves. Love seeks to unite, hate seeks to separate. And as biological human love is not compatible with complete identification with the object of its love except in the production of another self (child), so neither is hate compatible with total suppression, disparity and separation except in the destruction of another self (enemy).

And the same is true on a different level. For love is creative not only biologically but spiritually, and hate is destructive not only spiritually but biologically. And just as love works endlessly for creation and beauty and light, so does hate work endlessly for death, confusion and darkness. (An eastern philosopher tells us how in war the destroyed enemy still lives with the conqueror—still haunts him, remains with him in monuments, special days, speeches, and pledges and oaths of immolation. The slayer is also the slain, and "he whom I gave unto death was handed back to me in the immortality of the events." Hiroshima! Nagasaki!)

Love then is the highest reason.

Hate is ignorance in its worst form. And this is true at all times, whether in peace or war, in plenty or famine.

II

Now the beautiful is that which incites and excites the soul to love. I mean the truly beautiful.

There is no set or formal measurement or apt standard of beauty, for it varies with taste and time. But it never varies as to its inner power of giving pleasure to human beings, of giving true happiness.

Speech alive is poetry. And the more alive it is, the more poetic richness is in it.

Words so alive have the power to stir up, to move, to inspire in the reader the emotions with which they themselves are alive. And this gives pleasure.

(What is said of poetry is true of the other arts, the difference being only in the terminology proper to each.)

This receiving of pleasure is a process in appreciation, an

imaginative one. And art and poetry and literature are like chalices and abounding springs which hold life essentialized for the tasting and drinking and enjoyment as one feels and finds the need to so taste and drink. They are means of storing up the joy and richness of experience against the leakage and waste of time.

This intensification of beauty into art is nothing more than the enhancement, the intensification of the consciousness of beauty which is general and as far-reaching as mankind itself. And well that man might realize this glory, this divine gift and talent which he possesses! And woe to him when he does not, for the rust of battle shall consume his bones, and the timbers of his temples and market-places shall fall upon him with a great thunder!

III

Now in regard to the cruel, the disgusting, the fearful, and other such kindred subjects, why is art pleasing which deals with them? The answer is that in the treatment their "ugliness" disappears and they become sublimated and idealized with the emotion and intention of the artist who interpreted them. We view them as *his* representations of actuality and not as actuality itself. And the emotions and ideas aroused in us by the contemplation of these examples of art fill us and increase the abundance of our personality and are therefore pleasurable.

How is it possible to get pleasure out of witnessing or reading a tragedy, for instance? The answer seems simple, and is simple. For the spectator or reader is stirred to sympathy and pity for the tragic sufferer in whom he has grown interested, and a feeling of benevolence is aroused in him. And therefore the quality of mercy is doubly blessed.

The experience of sympathizing, of self-sacrificing, of giving unto another is pleasurable, pleasurable to the deeper and more spiritual self and is only unpleasurable to the shallower, more physical, less spiritual self.

Again, the urge to associate with, to help the suffering one, to lift him up, to ease him, protect him, brings with it not only the feeling but often the very picture or pictures of the completed association, and therefore a gained fullness of personality in this giving out results. Accordingly the feeling is pleasurable.

In tragedy, then, man's benevolent and unselfish self is called more strongly into play than not. And in giving, potentially and imaginatively (and rarely actually or factually) he the spectator the more completes himself therein and within. For such giving is born of love.

For love gives and hate takes away. Tragedy, then, arouses love. And the pleasure resulting therefrom is not a selfish or fearsome one at all—as Aristotle would seem to have us believe. In fact, the purgation or purifying he speaks of comes, and I think can only come, through this very unselfishness of giving, this love that loves to give.

Challenge to Citizenship

(Some Words to the Young People of North Carolina)

When Philip Amadas and Arthur Barlow, trusty captains for Sir Walter Raleigh out of England, came on the first expedition to Roanoke Island in 1584, they found a beautiful new world here. The air was enchanted with sweet odors and all around were "many goodly woods full of Deere, Conies, Hares, and Fowle." The trees were "the highest and reddest Cedars of the world," and the sandy shores were "so full of grapes, as the very beating and surge of the sea overflowed them."

Richard Hakluyt, the contemporary historian, writing about this part of the new world—which later became North Carolina—declared it to be "the goodliest land under the cope of heaven."

It was the goodliest land then, and now in these days of the present, looking out through my own home-hungry eyes, I too declare it still to be the goodliest land. If I am lovingly prejudiced, be it so, for I have lived long enough to know that home is home and without a home to rest his heart in a man is more lost than not.

Between that long-ago time and now—a stretch of nearly four hundred years—this Raleigh's Eden knew and suffered plenty of waste, frustration, anguish and despair—and worst of all self-degradation. Many of these evils and sorrows are still with us, too much so. But they are growing less year by year, I think, and to make them less and still less, to make these evils shrink away and the proper virtues of our hearts come forward and thrive in their place, an unrelenting dedication is necessary on our part, ceaseless and exciting effort is demanded. And the responsibility that this be a fact rests upon the shoulders and the minds and characters of all of us, especially on you young people coming on. For we older ones have about done our work, whatever of damage it was or of good it might be. And in the words of the usual commencement orator and moralist—even as we received the future from our forefathers out of the past, just so you must receive the future from us too and re-invigorate it with inspiration and strength for those that come after you.

Thus true progress is made or not and human lives are rich and full—or the more empty and dull.

After the early colonization attempts of Ralph Lane, of John White and Richard Grenville—all sharing in the knowledge and the propulsion of Sir Walter Raleigh's dream beyond the sea and all failing—this land of Carolina remained undisturbed for nearly a hundred years. It was still the goodliest land of fruits and flowers, of fish and animals, of thick shadow-laden forests and the furtive-footed red man. The despairing search for the Lost Colony ended in 1602 when Sir Walter sent his last expedition under Samuel Mace over to Roanoke Island. Mace like his predecessors, finding no trace of the settlers, loaded his ship with sassafras and cedar and returned to England, and their fate has remained a mystery to this day.

Queen Elizabeth died the following year, 1603, and Raleigh fell under the slovenly and cruel disfavor of James I.

His vision of a mighty stream of men and horses and ships moving, flowing toward the setting sun for the making of a new English nation perished with him under the headsman's axe. His holdings and interests in the new world had already been given over to the London Company. And the ships now being sent westward by that company shied away from the sucking shoals of Cape Fear and Hatteras and found haven in the deep waters of the Chesapeake. Thus Jamestown, Virginia, became the first permanent English settlement in America, and not Roanoke Island in North Carolina.

II

The years passed and Carolina continued a wilderness as it had been from time unending. Its bars and shallow sounds along the coast, its wayward winds and hurricanes were an effective barrier to any further effort at colonizing from the sea. Now and then a stray Indian trader ventured into this vast stretch of forest, and in 1709 John Lawson came exploring down from the west as far as New Bern to the east. In his history he gave a vivid account of the streams, of the hills, the plains and the tall trees waiting, waiting in a huge silence for the main coming of the white man. It was not until some years later that the religious-hounded and the religious-minded Scotch began to make their settlements along the jungled Cape Fear Valley. And there they sweated and prayed and cleared away the mighty sycamores, the sweetgums, oaks and pines to make their small farms and build their poor squatting cabins. Here they grazed their cattle, read and argued the Bible, distilled their brandy and kept a sharp and judgmenting eye upon the sins of their fellow men. In the meantime a scattering of English wastrels and wayward-footed fellows had progued on down the Currituck peninsula overland from the north out of Virginia and begun to spread their settlements around the shallow sounds and back up into the mainland.

Gradually small holdings of lands and Negroes were accumulated all along the eastern coastal plain. In the Piedmont region and mountains of the western part of the state, the Scotch-Irish, German and English settlers were moving down the valleys from Pennsylvania, Maryland and western Virginia to carry on the same sort of colonizing—but minus the Negroes.

In the east the development of the naval stores industry —if such an outdoor activity of tar, pitch and turpentine could be called an industry—increased the wealth of the people there and promoted the importing of more Negro slaves up from Charleston or through the port at Wilmington.

When this industry was exploited to near exhaustion, the inhabitants of the coastal plain returned to their farming, and by the middle of the nineteenth century had again established adequate but small free-holdings with here and there a larger house which might grudgingly be called a mansion. The settlers up in the hills westward continued as before with their little patches of crops, their heavy breeding of children, sermons and politics.

III

And then came the senseless horror of the Civil War. How far ahead of where she is today North Carolina would be but for that war, no one knows. And the same query would well fit any other Southern state. But certainly she would be far, far more advanced than she is. The slaughtering of the best of the young people of a state or nation can only cripple and deter the driving march of that state, that nation. It is true that out of this struggle came the abolition of slavery, but an awful price was paid for the righting of a wrong which reason long before should have righted. And what profit is there if in getting rid of one evil we have to commit a like or greater evil? Slavery and the war were both creations of irrationality, of prejudice and blindness, no matter what economic logic might claim.

But where there is no real leadership the people perish.

And thousands of North Carolina's young men lay dead on the battlefields, houses burned, property destroyed, and a horde of homeless, shiftless Negroes turned loose throughout the state. Not only that but a crazy social system was delivered unto us as a result of the catastrophe.

From the war a sort of caste system resulted, ill-defined but nevertheless real and devastating—the property owner, the poor white, and the Negro.

And during the long dead years after, a half century of them, these three classes lived in something of a desperate and turmoiling futility. Maybe these fifty years of uncreative living in North Carolina were necessary for what has finally followed—the surge of progress with which our hearts are now beginning to pulse and sing along. Maybe so, as the scientific historians can claim, but I still raise my lament and do not believe it.

But there is this value in it though, the value of remembrance. It is a sad story, these fifty years, and worth remembering in that we may the more judiciously, charitably and thoroughly carry on the great work in which we are now presently engaged.

During those fifty years the Negro remained at the bottom, and the sorriest North Carolina white man could say without getting up out of his splint-bottomed chair or shifting his wad of chewing tobacco in his jaw, "I'm better'n he is, for God so intended it to be," having reference thereby to the Scriptures which do say—as that old devout preacher down at Pleasant Union Church in Harnett County used to maintain to me—that Cain, son of Adam the first man, went up into the land of Nod and married a gorilla, and out of this union came the cursed and blighted Negro race. The poor white in North Carolina could never get so low that there wasn't somebody beneath him to look up to him and call him "mister." The helplessness and vomit-sick loneliness of nothing beneath were not so acutely known to him as to the black man. The Negro was at the bottom, and beyond him downward one could not go in the human scale.

No one looked up to the Negro in those years, unless it was the sticks and stones and beasts of the fields. And however kind they were in their insensitivity, they did not speak his language, they brought no comfort to his hurt heart. And in order to survive and keep his mind, he built himself a refuge in a world apart from social castes and evils and torments of the white man which his oppressor, by virtue of his oppression, felt no need to build. Ignorant and handicapped in goods and tools and instruments, he had to depend for inner realease and reaches of his imagination upon his own natural endowment as a human being. In this case it was his voice. It had to be his voice, for his hands were too busy otherwise in swinging the pick, in wielding the hoe, in showering down upon the axe—to help the white man build his roads, to lay the foundations for his banks, his colleges and his churches—into which last he the digger might not enter—and his factories. Dig and dig and dig, the song went. Dig this world in two, dig on to the setting sun, for they ain't no rising sun till I die!—

> "Look down, look down that lonesome road,
>   The hacks all dead in line,
>   Some give a nickel, some give a dime
>   To bury this poor body of mine."

The Negro learned to sing. His religion became a song, his life was eased by song. And out of his great need he produced an art—the Negro folksong and the spiritual. But he was unconscious of its meaning to the world out yonder, a world he did not know and one that in the main was ignorant of him.

But all was not lost to the ways of evil in those years. For freedom of the soul, the inner soul, won out of human bondage is the sweetest freedom of all. And from his suffering the Negro developed a dignity, a stoicism to evil and pain superior to that of his white neighbor and which now in these later days of his struggle for self-expression and free determination in the world are standing him in good stead.

But too much of his life was wasted in sheer fortitude. He had little time for anything else.

And as for the Negro's neighbor, the North Carolina poor white, he produced pretty much nothing through all those dreary years except himself. The narrow moralism of the Scotch settlers carried on in him, Methodist, Baptist, or Holy Roller, and he walked his lightless track with stinking shirt and unshaven face and one gallus plough-handle stoop, oppressed by the world and the strait-jacket of his religion. The juice and comedy of living were squeezed out of him, and he was left weazened-souled and dry-hearted as a shuck. The cramp of poverty, the clutch of ignorance, and the evil dreams of his lurid mind, gnarled him into bitterness. And when by some rare miracle of grace the tiny modest voice of true song or poetry or even a flower of beauty sprouted by his doorstep to waft its perfume along the sullen wind, he was instantly full of suspicion and ready to jeer it into silence or shrivel its bud with the spittle of his tobacco juice. As the Bible said, walk the straight and narrow path and let there be no too loud laughing, no unseemly shuffle of the dancing foot, no painted cheeks, no scarlet lips, no merry inviting fun-filled eyes. Remember the Sabbath day, to keep it holy, and the more empty and quiet and dead, the more holy it would be.

As for the third class of landlord, businessman, property owner—well, during those years the instinct for profits and power and exploitation was teased into full flush of activity in the situation in which he found himself. He was the banker, the lawyer, the storekeeper, the real estate man, the fertilizer dispenser, the mule and horse trader, the loan shark, the cotton and tobacco buyer, the installment merchant, the insurance agent, and patent medicine drug store vendor.

With pencil and paper and sometimes adding machines, and the mystic manipulation of numbers, the short term note, the long term note, the slap of good fellowship upon the shoulder, the intimate statement and devout affirmation of comradeship and trust and honesty, these men would gather their ten, their twenty, their thirty per cent from the Negro and the poor white, sweating them grievously in their bonds, even as they themselves were sweated by the big manufacturers and insurance men farther north in New York and New England. And year after year these poor ones would pay their toll from the lonely ploughman's furrow that led but to sickness and the grave.

True, from this energetic class of landlord, property owner, businessman, banker, there came some sort of progress for the state, but it was dearly won. Railroads were built with mules, hired-out convicts and a horde of underprivileged labor, black and white. And manufacturing and industry got something of a start—and got it on an average labor wage of less than $150 a year. Writing at that time, Walter Hines Pages, later ambassador to England under Woodrow Wilson, said that these men "held the country and all the people back in almost the same economic and social state in which slavery left them. There was no hope for the future under their domination. There would be no broadening of thought because only old thoughts were acceptable. No change in society, because society's chief concern was to tolerate no change. The whole community would stand still or slip further back."

And Holland Thompson, a native North Carolinian, envisioning a New South ahead, said—"Individuals of a type almost unknown in the South, though common in industrial societies generally, appear here and there. They are cold, shrewd, far-sighted. Sentiment in them does not interfere with the strict working of the principle of self-advantage."

And all the while going up and down the land and adding his evangelical and fervent blessing to ease the bondage in the status quo, went the hedge-priest of God, interlocutor and end man in one, talking of the wages of sin and the house not built with hands and the act of repentance and sobbing clamor at the mourner's bench, by which loud contrition all evil and all remembrance of former deeds of sin were wiped away. "For the end of those things is death. But now being made free from sin and become servants to God ye have your fruit unto holiness, and the end—everlasting life."

And thus the way was pointed to the place of main concern, the New Jerusalem in yonder world with its jeweled gates and its streets of gold where all tears were wiped away and grief was no more and where the angels lay around in the shade of the tree of life taking it easy and playing harps and singing their songs in praise of Jehovah. And all the while down below on earth, this goodliest land of ours was perishing in ugliness and decay.

But love and the secret getting of children went on

down here as they had since man began. Breasts burned with some ambition, hope flourished or died and envy too —just as always. The sun rose in its glory and set the same. The moon shone at night. The birds sang, and the raging summer storms tore the sky to tatters with their fearsome cannonading over Hatteras, over Rocky Mount, over Asheville, even as now. Drought and wind, storm, rain and wet weather, bud and leaf and winter-freeze were the same. Man walked among these wonders even as now, but he saw no glory in them. There was no poet's tongue to sing their praise.

IV

Then in the early years of this present century things began to change. The long drought of emptiness was broken, and some rain began to fall. Maybe the very length and severity of the drought helped it to come. We became shamefacedly conscious of that drought. Whatever the reason, new leaders began growing up in the state with a new point of view—men who saw the world with different eyes and saw the opportunities and challenges in that world. No doubt the coming of the machine age helped to bring this change to pass, though North Carolina had little or nothing to do with its coming. The initiative and energy of creative genius which produced it came from other states—in the north or middle west. In a single year soon after the Civil War, citizens of Ohio took out patents of fifteen hundred inventions—cornshellers, reaping machines, cash registers, adding machines, riding ploughs, guano distributors, hoisting cranes, machine tools, hydraulic presses, cranes, derricks, and the like. But in that same year, so far as I have been able to find out, not a single invention came out of North Carolina. But we prospered by these inventions, as they soon found their way into the state to help increase the production in our agriculture, in our infant commerce and in our beginning manufacturing plants.

Karl Marx says that the capitalistic Ephraim will never be parted from his idol of monetary profit except by force or revolution. Marx was wrong in this contention, I believe, as he was in many of his declarations of dialectical materialism. For with the new leadership in North Carolina in this twentieth century, there came also and however slowly a new attitude toward its people, its resources, its financial requirements—an attitude of cooperation and social responsibility.

One of the chief pioneers in this new view was Governor Charles B. Aycock. And for him the key to progress for the people of the state was education, not education for the few, but for all the people, white and black. He dreamed education, he preached education, he lived it. He went back and forth across the state, up and down the South, urging his blazing cause and proving it a practical need as he went.

"It is demonstrable that wealth increases as education of the people grows," he said. "Our industries will be benefited, our commerce will expand, our railroads will do a larger business when we shall have educated all the children of the state. It will be a glorious day for us if our people in the hour of prosperity and wonderful growth and development can realize that men can never grow higher and better by rising on the weakness and ignorance of their fellows, but only by aiding their fellows and lifting them to the same high plane which they themselves occupy." And in the last speech of his life, made at Birmingham, Alabama, in the spring of 1912, he was still strenuously urging the cause of universal education when he fell dead on the platform. The last word that came from his lips was the word—"education."

After Aycock came others likewise devoted to progress and a new order of things—among them Charles D. McIver, J. Y. Joyner, E. C. Branson, Josephus Daniels, Edward Kidder Graham, William Louis Poteat, Clarence Poe, and more lately Louis R. Wilson, Howard W. Odum, J. M. Broughton, Frank Graham, Gerald Johnson, S. H. Hobbs, Rupert Vance, Jonathan Daniels, Gordon Blackwell, Harriet Herring, Katharine Jocher, W. T. Couch, William T. Polk; and still more lately and especially, Benjamin Swalin, Robert Lee Humber, Albert Coates and W. A. Johnson.

V

And in the fields of finance, of commerce and industry, too, our bankers and manufacturing and political leaders —following the early civic-minded example of D. A. Tompkins—showed a new understanding of the state's problems and the need to solve them as keepers of the public weal. Relations between labor and capital improved, better wages and housing and health resulted. Production increased and markets were stimulated.

The families of Duke, Reynolds, Hanes, Gray, Cohn, Cannon and many others also began to work under a new and affirmative dispensation of cooperation. The time of heartless exploitation and callous disregard of human rights and requirements was going out of favor. Aycock's educational creed at last was being applied— "You cannot get the best for your boy and girl until you are ready to give the best to my boy and girl." True for millionaires, tenant farmers and factory workers alike.

And under this new guidance and leadership, North

Carolina moved forward. The story of that progress is apparent today all around us. And lucky for us it was, that when these fresh ideals of leadership came, we had to our hand and use the multitudinous and cunning products, gadgets and devices of the machine age with which to put them into practice. Maybe one helped produce the other, thus confirming again that all things work for good when cooperative men intend it.

For machinery is our universal and perfect servant. It is our physical emancipator. It speaks a single world-wide language and will serve alike all men of whatever color or creed or calling. Only brains are needed to know how to make it go. And brains are the common possession of all men, whether black, white or brown, with kinky hair or straight.

And with the dynamo, the airplane, the gas engine, the automobile, radio, movies, television, the bulldozer, the farm tractor, the microscope, the refrigerator, the diesel engine, the computer, atomic power, and a thousand other marvels man is finally subduing the world around him. Who could dare set a limit to what will yet be created, what will yet be understood—the cure for cancer, heart disease, the nature of light, gravitation, radiation and magnetism and matter, and the secret and control of life itself? And the greatest secret of all yet to be found out— the moral and social control of man himself?

Now is the best of all times to be alive in the world, the best time to be born, to be young, to be growing up and reaching ahead. And in this mighty adventure in the twentieth century, North Carolina is beginning to take her part. And our citizens now have a chance for creative and abundant living the like of which their parents and grandparents never had.

In these rich and productive recent years, we have seen the lonely poverty-stricken one-room log school house give way to modern consolidated education plants with good teachers, laboratories, books and modern facilities; seen our sandy and clay-mirey roads transformed into boulevards and hard surfaced highways; seen hospitals and colleges and churches rising in the land from Manteo to Murphy; our country homes painted and equipped with all up-to-date furnishings and conveniences; our cotton and tobacco farms mechanized and exuberant with strong and efficient labor; our bare and once eroded slopes growing green in the wintertime, and livestock and cattle adding profit and pleasure where once emptiness and marauding flourished to desolation; hydroelectric plants along our streams; modern factories in hamlet, town and city— whether of tobacco, textiles, furniture, machinery, electronics, synthetic fabrics, machine tools, steel fabrication, food and feed processing, boat-building, nylon-making, leather goods, woolens, pulpwood processing or whatnot; and home industries and weaving and handicrafts, potteries, wood carving and ceramics.

Here now is plenty of chance for all to roll up their sleeves, lift up their hearts and hands and clamorous voices, and go to it. Here is plenty of space to spread out in, to intensify our efforts—more than fifty thousand square miles of space. And these miles of earth are rich and mellow and fruitful and waiting to be made into an earthly garden. The climate is mild here, the rainfall is plentiful, and the sun is kind to man and beast and bird. And clay and wood and stone are all around with which to build our habitations and our homes. And lakes and running creeks and rivers and stretching forests are on every hand in abundance for all uses of joy and recreation.

VI

But what about one of the most important things of all? What about the art of living itself—living as an art? There is more to existence than the creation of foods and services, of barter and trade, of growing crops and selling them. In every man there burns a primal impulse, an urge to the making of a more pleasing and beautiful world.

A good house, a good car, good roads, money in the bank, a satisfaction of physical needs, food, clothing, shelter, security against want—these are blessings, virtues even. These must and usually do come first, first in time if not in final significance. These are practical necessities now. But they only prepare the way for what is of greater value—a truly good and noble and cultural living. And for this last—beauty, harmony, symmetry and strength of soul as well as health and comfort of body are necessary.

I believe that the arts—literature, poetry, music, drama, architecture, philosophy, true science, criticism, painting, sculpture, dancing—are the warmth and glory of life and the essential virtues of a civilization. And we are beginning to wake up to our lack in these forms and to do something about them too. The state is finally taking cognizance of the theatre, of book-publishing, of painting, of sculpture, and making appropriations to encourage them. Instance the Carolina Playmakers, the North Carolina Symphony, the art gallery at Raleigh, and the University Press at Chapel Hill. Aesthetic and imaginative recreational programs are being organized throughout the state. With the leisure and easy means of communication and travel and get-together provided by this our machine age, our people are more and more taking an interest in their traditions—memorializing the best of our past in school plays, outdoor dramas, in historical novels, in celebrations, in orations, in essays and in the work of historical societies and groups.

The state is at last producing some writers. The work of our women's book and literary clubs is acting as a great stimulation for creative production. Our different colleges are establishing courses, giving college credit for imaginative work in writing, in painting, in music and the kindred arts.

Everywhere about us is felt an upward lift in our civilization. But it is in the main only felt, it is just beginning.

Consider that the only great painter North Carolina has ever had came to us on Roanoke Island in 1585 in the person of John White. And when he returned to England he left the state without an important artist of the brush to fill his place to this day—a stretch of those same four centuries mentioned above.

And not until O. Henry and Tom Wolfe came along did this state produce any story-tellers of prime excellence. We have never produced a first-rate musician or composer, no first-rate philosopher nor critic nor essayist, no first-rate scientist or statesman—that is, first-rate enough to help mold and influence the course of the world's history, no supremely great poet, singer, dancer, actor, or dramatist.

But we will produce them. In time we will. For we have the stuff in our people out of which to develop and grow them. And the opportunity and encouragement are here.

VII

For all our roll-call of accomplishments, then, and things done, we actually have got only a little way along.

While we have been making this great material and some cultural progress, other states and sections also have been taking their strides forward. Most of them, except for a few in the southeastern region, have far out-distanced us.

There are a million children going to public schools each year in North Carolina, and this would be joyful news to Governor Aycock. But it would be sad news for him to learn that two thirds of them drop out before they ever finish high school and less than one out of fifteen ever finish college. This is an enormous casualty list along the way. And compare these figures with those of any New England or middle-western state. Here we stand, or rather lie, forty-seventh in the nation.

So, after all these wonderful years and in spite of Aycock and his followers, we still are near the bottom among the states in, of all things, education. And the same is true in per capita income, and in wages paid, in farm income, in old age benefits, in books and magazines read, in money spent for health, in dentists and doctors, and on and so on. We still import butter, milk, apples, eggs, beef, pork, shoes, tools, and dozens and dozens of other things which we should raise or make ourselves—at a cost annually of more than three hundred millions of our hard-earned dollars.

And here are some of the saddest statistics of all. There is a constant and heavy drainage of migration out of our state that shows no signs of stopping. We lose more than fifty thousand of our best skilled workers and artisans every year who go to seek better opportunities elsewhere. And every year more than sixty thousand of our finest young high school and college people, our best brains and talents, move away from the state. These are the very people from whom our further cultural and spiritual as well as material progress must come.

Of course their talents and abilities are not lost in the

body of the republic. But as I said before, home is home and a man has to have a home to function at his best. He has to belong to be at his creative best. The tearing up of roots and getting started elsewhere afresh often require too much psychic dislocation. It is my belief that if the young people of North Carolina stayed at home and worked where they are, brought their best gifts to bear on the problems and challenges here, their lives would be more fruitful and rich in joy and results both for themselves and society around them. We must somehow keep them in North Carolina. We must find ways to offer them a full and exciting and dramatic chance for living, and they must learn how to find it, to accept it and stay here and create.

VIII

Now why do we, why does the South, for all our attainments, continue to lag behind in these things? Why are we always in the rear rank, even stragglers, in the march of the nation's progress? No doubt there is a whole concatenation of reasons, but I think the foremost reason of all is our unrealistic and impractical attitude toward the Negro. Say that this is not a reason but a result of a long-past custom of social living. That is to make no explanation. For a result in a chain of events always becomes in turn a cause for a succeeding result. And I believe our treatment of the Negro continues to be the real source of our comparative economic and cultural poverty.

This minority group constitutes about one-third of our total population below the Mason-Dixon line. It simply is not possible, no matter how much we court northern industry and seek new sources of revenue—it is not possible for us to build a thriving state and region when so vast a number of our people are discriminated against and denied full privileges for self-expression and growth. How could a railroad bridge, say, be strong if one third of the piers that held it up were weak? How could a football team win victories if a third of its members were crippled and hamstrung? So it is with any institution, state or nation. It is a matter of obvious addition and subtraction to say so, to know so.

In this beloved state of ours since its first permanent settling nearly three hundred years ago, some ten to twelve millions of Negroes—human beings—have lived and died. And out of that number who could make even a brief roll-call of individuals who have developed their lives to anything like their full capabilities? Where are our even adequate Negro scientists, our Negro poets and composers, our philosophers, doctors, physicists, novelists, engineers, agriculturists, botanists, lawyers, architects, educators, manufacturers? There have been a few, a pitiful few, who by almost superhuman effort and against every difficulty have been able to emerge out of their poverty to a bit of local prominence. Think of the appalling loss, the waste!

Today the per capita income of the Negro in North Carolina is around one-half of that of the white man. That means his earning power is just that and his purchasing power the same. Think what potential markets are gone with that lost income and likewise taxes for schools, hospitals and roads. And money, cries the frustrated governor and legislators, is so desperately needed!

Is it because the Negroes are by race inferior in their hearts and minds and abilities that they have failed so? Of course not. The myth of innate racial superiority has been exploded long ago. It is all a matter of environment and opportunity. The Negroes are a great and gifted people. They are our people. They are us! But through these long years they have had no proper chance. They have been kept down, hindered, suppressed.

And even now in these days of world revolution and release of human aspirations elsewhere—aspirations fired often into actions by our own philosophy of government—in Asia, Africa, in the Middle East—the political leaders in North Carolina and in most of the Southern states as well are still determined to keep the Negroes in what they call their place. What ignorance, what piteous stupidity!

Obviously the real wealth of a state or a nation lies ever in the talents of the people themselves—all the people irrespective of race, color, or kind. Should we not then work to release these talents and energies here in North Carolina, here in the South, encourage them to grow rather than trying to stifle them? For if we did so, then this region would in time be not the poorest section in the nation as it is today, but the richest—richest in all the good and creative things of life.

Yes, the time has come for us, for you young people, to get busy as citizens, as patriotic Americans, on this matter especially. We have been too slow, we have too long delayed in honestly tackling this problem of race relations. We have slid around it. And now that the Federal Supreme Court has spoken the law of the land, the imperative to do our duty is clearer and stronger than ever. We must change our outlook and our practice. Common sense, true religion, sound science, the drift of the age, the bent of the modern world, demand it. We can no longer afford to be a party to this prejudiced withholding of the economic and social blessings of our democracy from so great a number of our people. We must make our political faith a living fact—living not for some of our people but for all the people. To refuse to do so is to be betrayers of the very

principles which gave this nation its birth and inspired its
growth. And these principles are as vital and compelling
today as ever they were—nay, more compelling than ever.

IX

As you know from your history teachings here, our
government was founded on the basic concept that all men
are created equal—not equal in talent, in wealth and
quantitative strength, but equal in the soul, equal in their
inviolate right and claim to justice, to fair play, to opportunity. Thomas Jefferson set this down as the prime truth,
the first ideal, in the Declaration of Independence. And
again and again our founding fathers in their writings, in
their speeches, affirmed and reaffirmed that ideal—Washington, Franklin, Adams, Hamilton, Mason, Madison, and
others.

The principles growing out of this moral intuition
were later summed up and put forth in a shining roll-call
in the bill of rights of our Federal Constitution—"Freedom
of religion, of speech, of the press, of the right of the
people peaceably to assemble and to petition the government for a redress of their grievances, security of a people
in their person and property, due process of law, habeas
corpus, trial by jury, and freedom from slavery and servitude as becomes free men."

These are the constituents then, the elements of moral
and social strength, the ancient but ever-lasting truths
that have gone into the making of our philosophy of government—the righteous doctrine out of which our ideal,
our American dream, has manifested itself forth in a great
republic and which today demands of you the best that you
have to give.

And I believe you will give that best. I believe you

will no longer be willing to share in the failures of this state and region, share in the guilty responsibility of cruel repressions now practiced among us. You will want to, will be eager to give of your full talent and strength in helping bring this country into a final and fine flowering of waiting greatness—a nation of justice, truth, courage and cooperation among men.

The time is now, the place is here.

Then to work. And as we all work and sing and pull together, we shall at last make for all our people, rich and poor, black and white, high and low, this beloved North Carolina what it ought to be and will be in truth and deed —"the goodliest land under the cope of heaven."

Such is the challenge, such the opportunity open to you.

Again the Southern Negro

(An Old-Time Philosopher Talks)

I

My old friend the miller has definite ideas on a lot of subjects including the Southern Negro. One day I was sitting with him in his mill-house, as I often did, helping him shell his yellow corn, when he turned to me and said, "What is the biggest mistake this country ever made?"

I thought awhile and then said I didn't know, unless it was the Civil War. That had seemed to me a useless and tragic thing.

"No doubt about that being a mistake, all right," he said, "with its killings and destruction, but it weren't the biggest by a long shot."

"No?"

"No. For the biggest was the bringing of the Negro to our shores, and I reckon the Civil War was the final result of that too, come to think of it. Look about you. Everywhere you turn we are reminded of our mistake. Just before you drove up in your car, Fannie Privett and her seven mullatto young'uns come dragging by begging for a peck of meal. I gave it to her, and she went on down the road to her cabin, with her kids plundering and proguing in the edge of the woods hunting for bullaces, 'simmons, pinemast, and anything else they could pick up. And there's not only one family like that in this neighborhood but several. And what do they do? Why they all marry—or not—and breed like rabbits over the land, adding to our mommick and misery. From Texas to Baltimore you will find them like that—traipsing, drabble-tailed people living on the scum and picking the garbage of the world. Oh, yes, the orators and you writers and teachers keep preaching and talking a lot about what a great thing freedom has been for the Negro race. I wonder. The truth is, they're not free. And we the white men are not free either. They pull us down on every hand, and as we pretend to try to pull them up."

"But we don't pretend," I replied. "We actually do. Look at the school buildings we're putting up for them—the education, the better health." I would often argue with the miller mainly to hear what he would say.

"What education, what better health?" he asked irritably, and then went on. "Take my Tom mule. I keep him fat, curry him, look after him, and he does my work, and he helps produce his own feed besides. Suppose I said to him, 'Tom, I'm Abraham Lincoln, in this year of our Lord 1862, and I'm going to set you free. No more gall of trace chains, of collar sores and sweating in the summer fields. No.' So I open the stable door and lot gate and say, 'Get out. You're a free mule. You're on your own, and root hog or die.' And out goes Tom kicking up his heels, feeling free and happy as a lark, jolly as a doodle-bug. But what happens to Tom? He winds up like the Negro—yeh—hard up, down in the dry reed swamp or in a briar patch. And if he's got any sense he'll be back at my lot gate soon braying for me to take him in, ready to get back into the harness and do what I tell him. Yes, we say we've freed the Negro. And what has he got out of it? I'll tell you—his one gallus, his plough-handle, his digging at the bottom, his poor wages, flies and hovels, dysentery and disease. That's the sort of thing he's got. Go up there in town and talk to Dr. Rainer. He'll tell you. Let him show you his files."

"I know there's that side to it," I said, "but that's not all. You forget their music, the work of certain individuals like Booker T. Washington, like Carver, like—Paul Robeson, like—"

"It's enough," he jeered. "What I'm getting at is this —if we're going to free him, let's do it. Do you know what the average pay for Negro cooks is in this Harnett County neighborhood?"

"No, I don't."

"Well, being as you're always writing about the Negro you ought to look into it. It runs from five to six dollars a week—and I mean a week of fifty-five or sixty hours too —with an old hand-out dress now and then or a moldy hambone thrown in. Now is any mother of a household, black or white, that works for such a wage free and self-respecting? I ask you?"

"Well, it's pretty poor wages, that's true. But the people aren't able to pay more."

"Who said they weren't able to pay more?"

"They do—the people."

"If they'd all get together and decide to pay more, they could."

"But how are they going to get together? Our economy is geared to—"

"That's just it—let them decide to do it and stick to it —fight on back up the line to their own wages above. If the politicians spent as much time really trying to cooperate on such things in this country as they do talking about individualism, and freedom and the American way of life, they'd get somewhere. Take all these speeches of Henry Wallace—no, I won't go into that. I tell you when this war and world of evil has faded from the battlefields, this country's got to do something about revising its Declaration of Independence and its Constitution—especially its Constitution, since I reckon it's too late to change the Declaration. We've got to do something about capital and labor, set forth the place and meaning of each, and we've got to do something about this Negro business."

"That's exactly what Mr. Wallace says."

"But we've got to apply commonsense to it and not the dole or some WPA idea that he and the President talk about. You can't subsidize people into being good citizens and self-reliant souls that way. The only way is for them to earn what they deserve and what they get—give 'em a chance to earn it. Yessir, the poor old South is cursed from Sodom to Gomorrah by the Negro and our mishandling of him. Just suppose we didn't have any Negroes among us—what a different people we'd be!—stronger, better brains, characters, better everything. They're ruining us and we're ruining them. We keep them in the ditch, the briar patch and the swamp, and in keeping them there we have to stay with them."

"What would you do—send them back to Africa?"

"Of course you can't send them back to Africa. They're here with us—citizens, such as they are, with their rights, privileges, and responsibilities. So I say if we're going to meet the problem we've got to do it in a wholehearted, commonsense manner. We've got to use authority over them, the way I do over Tom. We've got to be clear-headed and hard. Yes, you heard me—hard as well as fair."

"That sounds a little like Fascism or Nazism, doesn't it?"

" I don't care what it sounds like," he answered abruptly, "just so it makes sense. There's no sense in the way we're running things now. You know that. You spoke of education and schools. Look what we do there. We put up two school buildings where we ought to put up only one. Why? Because one has to be for the black man and his sun-burnt relatives and another has to be for the white man and his prejudice. Why? Is there a white education and a black education? Is knowledge a matter of color? Our glorious old commonwealth seems to think so, for a colored woman can hold an A certificate and a white woman the same certificate, and the state says the white woman's is worth more than the colored's, and the pay check is made out accordingly. Seems to me Jefferson and the founding fathers talked a lot about equal [1] abilities having a chance at equal rewards. If the American way of life that everybody beats their gums about don't mean that, what does it mean? No, sir, we act just like, say, there was a Negro multiplication table and a white folks' table, and like two times two is four for some people and three and a half for others. Does that make sense? For instance, if we build a bus station we've got to go to the expense of building two waiting rooms, white and colored. Every filling station has to have its four separate restrooms—for white men and white women, for Negro men and Negro women. And down in Robeson County they've got six—for the Indian, the Negro and the whites. No wonder they all stay so dirty. It's too expensive to keep 'em clean. And every railroad station has its separate places for the races to stand and look at each other through the bars, breeding suspicion and night-time trouble. There's no sense in that. It don't add up to the truth."

"Then you mean the solution is race equality?"

"That's the question they always raise up—the old question of race equality, and whether I'd want my daughter to marry a black man. Equality depends on the character of the individuals concerned and is not a matter of laws and iron bars. That's the way I see it. And as for the marrying

[1] Salaries have been equalized since this was written.

matter, I ain't got a daughter. If I did have, I'd say let her take care of that when it came up. The thing to deal with is what's before us now—the mess and waste and degeneration we've got into. And to do that we've got to be honest, got to get up manhood enough to face this thing, wipe out these barriers and double dealings, put the Negro on his own, give him a chance to be a man as he wants to be, a chance to earn a decent living, raise his wages, let him in the labor unions, give him a chance in politics, a vote, a say-so in public affairs, let him become a real citizen with a country he belongs to and one that belongs to him. And he'll rise up to meet his opportunity then. He'll become somebody, sure as shooting. That's the way humanity behaves and always will no matter what the place, the color, the creed, or previous condition of servitude our big-mouth governor speaks about. And if we do that, then I won't have the insult of such old hussies as this one that's just been here coming up to me and saying and begging in a whining voice, 'Please suh, gimmie a little meal for me and my poor chillun—gimmie suh!' If that means race equality, then I'm for it. Yes, sir, this country's made a lot of mistakes. It was a mistake to fight the war of 1812. The Civil War was a grievous mistake. Going over there into Asia and putting our fingers into the Philippine pie and our head in the kindly open door of China was a mistake. We oughta got it hung in the crack, and by golly sometimes it looks like we did. The Monroe Doctrine was a mistake, narrow-minded and one-sided, saying 'you can't play in my front yard but I'm going to play in yours.' Yessir. But the greatest mistake of all was when our forefathers brought the Negroes to this country. Now let's get busy and wipe out this mistake."

"I agree with you. We ought to do it—"

"Yes, I know you do," he replied, "from the books you

write I'd know that. But you're like too many of the folks down here—too talky, easy, and wishy-washy. You've got to quit talking and go to work on the problem—be hard, put your foot down, be scientific about it, as they say up at your university. Yessir, use authority and the strong hand, discipline, cut out this soft Santa Claus stuff."

"You're right," I said.

"You're dang right I'm right," he said.

II

A wagon turned in from the highway and came knocking across the mill yard toward us. The old man looked out through the open door and held his ear of corn still for a moment in his hand. I followed his gaze and saw a bent-over young Negro man sitting on the wagon seat draped in an old shawl and pulled along by a poor shaky and raw-bony mule.

"There you are again," said the miller gesturing with the ear of corn and then beginning to shell it rapidly with the butt of his palm. "That's Claude Young bringing his corn to be ground. He's half-paralyzed from a bad blood disease. Some low-down woman has hamstrung him and burnt his life away. Every time I see him his tongue's a little stiffer and his words harder to understand. Now ain't that a fix for a young fellow to get into? No telling how many colored girls he's contaminated too."

"Yes, it's bad," I said dolefully.

"Somebody ought to put the law on him and make him get cured up— Slam a pistol in the small of his back and march him to a doctor, if you have to," said the miller.

"I sent him to Dr. Rainer once myself," I said, "but he didn't go back."

"Hah, there you are!" the old man exclaimed, throwing out his hands in moody irritation.

The wagon drew up in front of the door, and the Negro made a blubbering heigh-oing noise in his throat.

"Wait a minute, son," the old miller called out suddenly and kindly, "We'll help you with that heavy sack!"

The two of us went out and lifted down the bag from the wagon. And the Negro Claude sat aloft and silent in his seat, his face cryptic, tragic, and expressionless.

"How're you feeling, Claude?" I asked.

"Po'ly, Mitha Paul," he managed to answer, still staring lightlessly before him.

Beyond the rim of pines that skirted the millpond to the west the autumn sun was going down in a splurge of violent color, dyeing the world and sky high and wide with its flame. Like a great fiery eye it was going down, and for an instant it seemed to peer out at me with a mocking jaundiced gleam.

"We'll have your meal in a jiffy, Claude," the old miller called cheerily. And Claude sat bent like a crooked stump snag under his ragged shawl, saying nothing, saying nothing at all as we two Southern theorists got busy serving him.

And while I watched his corn a-grinding, a lump kept rising in my throat, the lump that rises in the throat of the soft indulgent South. (God help my land or anywhere when the steel of machinery and the governor's industry and cold statistics take that lump away!) And I grieved over his crippled and spoiled young life, seeing him so quiet and waiting there, so lonely and so humble, ignorant and lost there under the great down-bending sky. Nothing but sympathy and love could I feel for him, and neither blame nor anger at all for any of his sins and wild misdoings.

Then we carried his meal back to him.

"Claude," I finally said, "you'll have to go with me up to see Dr. Rainer again tomorrow."

"Etha, Mitha Paul," he mumbled meekly.

He understood and I understood—he my suffering care for him and I his gentle meekness. And because it was so I felt a little glad, and I knew he was glad. And the final wink of the wise all-seeing sun was not so mocking any longer now, as the huge thumb of the tree-dark hill extinguished it. And I was glad too to remember suddenly that I had forgot all about authority and the case of stern redeeming law; for the moment I had.

The boy dragged on his rope reins, stirred a bit painfully in his seat, and drove slowly and knockingly away.

"We'll work these things out down here somehow," I said, half into the air and half to distant human ears— "somehow we will."

"I hope so," said the old miller resignedly.

And standing there silent we watched the ramshackle wagon fade away in the sweet enfolding gloom.

Art and Religion

Art like religion is universal and infinite, and every man shares in it according to his ability and desires. This is true of the smallest man and the proudest, the best and the worst. In appreciation all men are artists more or less, and in the creation of beauty the same is true. But some men possess such desires and abilities to a greater degree, and these—as they express themselves in outward tokens and forms—are generally given the name "artists;" whereas those of weaker sensibilities, gifts and practices are usually understood to be outside that category. The artist as such is one who by the skillful use of symbols transmits his feelings, ideas, and vision to others in such a way that their appreciation of themselves and the world is heightened.

Discrimination of values is necessary in judging the art object and likewise the artist. By agreement of tradition and individual testimony some creations of artistic genius are greater than others. Therefore even in the universality of the subject-matter and its applicability, the man of judgment must distinguish the better from the worse, the higher from the lower. And at once we are led into the age-old problem of morality and art. But this is a difficulty to be solved, not a discouraging answer to be accepted, and in simple words the answer is—that the higher the art the more it ennobles; the lower, the more it degrades. Apart from aesthetic history, most of us know the truth of this

contention by our own experiences. Barbaric and voluptuous
music, blatant military bands, a clamorous ritual of the
evangelist, often achieve an immediate and disastrous effect
by drowning all judgment and common sense, so that the
participant is a prey to the cheap mood and meaning of the
occasion. On the contrary an Aeschylean tragedy, a symphony of Beethoven, the heroic figures of Michelangelo,
may serve to exalt us and at the same time stir our powers
of feeling and reason to a more complete unity of vision
and purpose. By common consent of statistical philosophy,
proofs in endless number could be adduced concerning the
moral and immoral power of art. But no amount of mathe-
matics can help us in deciding what we need to feed our
spirits upon. The ancient commandment of adhering to the
good and growing away from the bad is generally good
enough for our purpose.

But how shall one specifically distinguish between the
good and the bad in art? This is a metaphysical question
to most of us and is usually put away from consideration by
a typical and dogmatic answer that "if I like a thing it is
good, if I dislike it it is bad—for me." This individual and
democratic judgment is an old story and an easy escape
for one not bothered over-much with either curiosity or
the cat. If X says that the "St. Louis Blues" is a fine piece
of music simply because he likes it, he is in the main making
a subjective and quantitative valuation. If another person
says he dislikes this composition and thinks it bad because
it outrages his feelings—he too is guilty of the same sort of
judgment.

Though these views are not entirely false, they err in
being piecemeal and partial. The old I-like-it or I-like-it-not
philosophy of a George Jean Nathan, say, is not sufficient
if one would continue the stretches of his reason for longer
than a mood, a moment, or a day. For suppose that one

who likes the "St. Louis Blues," is a man of naïve emotions whose judgment is simple and untrained, who has experienced little in what men have agreed upon as civilization, culture; and suppose that the second person, say, is a Brahms —then the chance are that the judgment of the second person is nearer the truth we are seeking than that of the first—though often X the peasant may discern a kind of quantitative, a small and immediate beauty which the sophisticated, the wider-ranged man will miss.

However, the fact that the subject falls into this double question of good and bad proves that a subjective judgment is not sufficient in itself, and that the judgment of the judger is to be considered in weighing the validity of his conclusions. In distinguishing the better art from the worse, then, we must decide between the better appreciator and the worse, and to do so leads us to the necessary conclusion that there is an objective standard in aesthetic considerations as well as a subjective one. Now the objective and subjective phases of the matter are not antagonistic; in fact they become one in the complete aesthetic experience.

Consequently in judging a better or worse work of art, we must inquire as to its effect upon ourselves both in terms of ourselves and the external world, and likewise we must so value the creator himself. This returns us to the definition given above. To repeat, we must consider what the work of art, the play, the moving picture, the novel, the symphony, makes us feel and think about our world, ourselves, and about our fellowman. In an immediate aesthetic experience these questions do not always obtrude themselves, but they necessarily follow upon that experience, contemplatively follow if the experience is valid and real. In an honest search of ourselves we will find the old truth—that a good or noble work of art heightens our pleasure in and adherence to the Good; that is, each one under its spell re-affirms in himself the desire and finer purpose of his life, and stands ever stronger in the gripping certainty of an absolute reality and meaning to his existence and that of others like him and in the determination—in Aeschylean phrase—that the right shall prevail. In this, art and religion are one and stand opposed to the pessimisms of any science whatsoever.

Foreword to The Lost Colony

Back in 1921 when I was a student at the University of North Carolina and trying to turn out one-act plays fast enough to equal the measure of Professor Frederick Koch's inspiration, I got to thinking about the story of Sir Walter Raleigh's long-ago tragic lost colony as subject matter for a play. So I decided to go down to remote, at that time, Roanoke Island on the Atlantic coast and look around at the original site of the colony settlement. I set out from Chapel Hill and traveled by bus and train to Beaufort, thence up Pamlico Sound by mailboat, and finally made the latter part of my journey across the open inlet by hiring a fisherman and his little motorboat—in all a distance of some three hundred miles. I still remember that fisherman, a muscular old fellow, sturdy and craggy and coming back to me now in visualization like that old man Ernest Hemingway wrote about recently in his great sea story. He sang a song to me as we went across. I still can remember some of the words—

> "Oh, haul away, bully boys,
>   Oh, haul away high-o,
> We'll wipe away the morning dew
>   And then go below."

It was night when I arrived at the little town of Manteo on the island. I got a room at a local boardinghouse, and early the next morning started walking up the sandy road through the forest toward the place known as Fort Raleigh four miles away. I plodded along in the ankle-deep sand, and the sun was coming up in its great and fearsome flame when I got to the little grove of pines and live-oaks on the edge of Croatan Sound and stood beside the small squat stone erected by a local historical group in 1893 to Virginia Dare, the first English child born in the new world. This stone was the only mark to tell that this was Fort Raleigh and the site of the perished colony. I wandered around in the woods. I idly plucked some sassafras twigs and chewed them, and thought upon that band of hardy pioneers who, three hundred and thirty-four years before, had come to this spot to build a fort, a bastion, a beachhead for the extension of the English-speaking empire across the sea. In a holly tree a mocking bird trilled his timeless note.

I thought of the hardships that these people had suffered, of the dark nights, the loneliness, the despair and frustration here, desolate and forgot by Queen Elizabeth in her concern with her Spanish war in England faraway. In my mind I could hear the cries of the sick and hungry little children, see the mothers bending above their rough home-made cribs as their little loved ones twisted and turned in their fever and their fret. And what anguish, what heartache and home-sickness! And ever the anxious expectant look toward the eastern sea where never the bright sail of a ship was seen nor the mariner's cheer was heard, to tell that help was nigh. Night after night, day after day, only the murmur of the vast and sheeted waters, only the sad whispering of the dark forest to break upon their uneasy dreams.

Yes, here on the very spot where I stood, all this suffering and pain had happened, all this had been endured.

II

I came away charged with inspiration to write a drama on the lost colony. Back in Chapel Hill I promised "Proff," as we all affectionately called Professor Koch, to have a piece for his playwriting class come the next week. I turned out a one-acter for production in the University Forest Theatre. It told an imaginary story of Virginia Dare and how she grew up and lived in the wilderness among the Indians, falling in love with Chief Manteo's son and marrying him—a forest idyll. But the class didn't think much of it. Proff Koch didn't care for it either, though he smiled and said it had good points. That was his way—always trying to find some ground for encouraging a student. By that time I thought it was pretty rotten. Somewhere along the line my inspiration had petered out. I had come home and started reading too much in the literature of the subject, I guess. One piece that had stuck in my mind was a long poem by a North Carolina author which told the made-up legend of how Virginia Dare, as a beautiful young woman, had been turned into a white doe by the spell of an angry Indian suitor and how she had been mistakenly shot by the arrow of her own true lover, another Indian brave—only returning to her beautiful maidenly self in the throes of death. So I remember it.

I threw the play away, and turned back to writing furiously about the poor whites and the Negroes of my native county in Eastern North Carolina.

III

Ten years later I was teaching philosophy in the University of North Carolina. One day there came a knock on my office door and W. O. Saunders, of Elizabeth City,

North Carolina, entered. Saunders was the editor of an active paper in his town known as the *Independent*. At that time he was famous locally, not for his editorship of a liberal and outspoken paper or as a contributor of articles to *Collier's Magazine*, but for his recent pioneer activity of walking up and down Broadway in New York City in the mid-heat of summer, wearing pajamas and carrying a sign advocating a change to sensible summer clothing for the comfort of the American male.

Saunders explained to me that he had been in Germany some months past and had seen the great Bavarian outdoor religious play at Oberammergau.

"Paul," he said, "we've got to have something like that in North Carolina. And I've got an idea."

Then he went on to say that the story of Sir Walter Raleigh's lost colony, he thought, would make a good drama. "I hear you've already written something about it," he said.

I told him I had tried a piece on Virginia Dare, but it hadn't worked out.

"You see," he said, "1937 will soon be here. This will mark the 350th anniversary of the colony and the birth of Virginia Dare also. We ought to have a great exposition—something like the Jamestown Exposition of 1907. We could move a tribe of Indians down to Roanoke Island, let them carry on farming, raise tobacco, set their fishing weirs, just the way they did at the time Sir Walter sent his colony over. We could have every man on the island grow a beard and the people could wear the dress of three centuries ago." He got excited, his eyes shone. "It would be the biggest thing ever to hit North Carolina," he said. "We would get nation-wide, world-wide publicity for it."

We talked some more and finally agreed to have a meeting down in Manteo. The date was set for three weeks later, and my wife and I drove down there overland, and in the crowded courthouse the project of doing a drama was initiated. The idea of a full-blown exposition seemed by this time to be too ambitious an undertaking. Also we were realizing that the Carolina fishermen wouldn't take to the idea of growing beards and wearing doublet and hose.

W. O. Saunders made a speech that night. I made a talk. But the audience still seemed rather cold and unenthusiastic. Suddenly from the back of the hall a bell-like voice rang out, the voice of United States Senator Josiah William Bailey. He and Lindsay Warren, who was then a Congressman and later became Comptroller General of the United States, were down at nearby Nags Head on a fishing expedition. They had come over to the courthouse meeting and sat in the back unrecognized. Now Senator Bailey got up, strode down the aisle and delivered a speech that soon had everybody eager for activity. He made it quite clear to us that Roanoke Island was the true inspiration for Shakespeare's play, *The Tempest*. And then he fell to quoting in a voice that sent the chills running up and down our backs—

> " 'Come unto these yellow sands,
>   And then take hands,
>   Court'sied when you have and kiss'd,
>   (The wild waves whist,)
>   Foot it featly here and there,
>   And sweet sprites the burden bear.
>   Hark, hark!' . . . .

> " 'Full fathom five thy father lies,
>   Of his bones are coral made,
>   Those are pearls that were his eyes;
>   Nothing of him that doth fade,
>   But doth suffer a sea-change
>   Into something rich and strange.
>   Sea-nymphs hourly ring his knell,
>   Hark now I hear them—ding-dong bell.' "

"When Shakespeare wrote 'Come unto these yellow sands,' " he went on, "he had in mind the sands of Roanoke Island. No doubt about it. The tragedy of the lost colony that happened on this island inspired the pen of the immortal Shakespeare to write one of his finest and most imaginative plays. This is a sacred spot here, people. Let us put on a drama, our drama, here at this patriotic shrine where those brave pioneers lived, struggled and died. Yes, let us tell their story to the world."

We enthusiastically voted to do it.

IV

After this, committees were set up, meetings held, and the Roanoke Island Historical Association was reactivated.

One of the meetings I especially remember. It was in Raleigh, and the governor and a number of legislators were present. The newly-appointed promotion man arrived with a Hollywood-looking secretary on each arm and a big scrolled map drawn up, which he exhibited triumphantly, showing the whole of Roanoke Island's thousands of acres of land cut up in lots all numbered and ready for sale. We had to get rid of him.

And I felt the old feeling of that early summer morning ten years before, coming back to me. A group of North Carolina and Norfolk, Virginia, businessmen agreed to raise the necessary funds for building the amphitheatre and producing the play. I got busy writing it.

This time let me hold true to the stimulation of my subject matter. Let me keep ever before me the sense and image of this group of tragic suffering people—more than a hundred and twenty of them—men, women and children who had fared forth from England on that fatal day in 1587 to brave the turmoil and terror of the vast and raging sea in search of their destiny, these the keepers of a dream. Away with all secondhand sources—let it come prime, let it come raw.

And I would forget the baby Virginia Dare except as one of the items in the whole dramatic symphony. Don't worry because the father's name Ananias must cause a dramatic emphasis different from that of history. These didn't matter. The main thing was the people. For these were the folk of England, the folk of our race—these who had come to labor here with their hands to wrest from cryptic nature her goods and stores of sustenance, or die, these who had to live with their feet in the earth and their heads bare to the storms, the wind and sleet and the falling fire from heaven. Flood and drought and hunger were their lot, their minds and spirits a prey to the nightmare fear and horror of the dark and impenetrable wilderness around them.

And yet out of this testing, this straining and tension here on these lonely shores, this being hammered on an anvil of God, there must emerge the faith that lay native in them as workers, as believers, as spiritual beings who raised their eyes in awe to the great Presence riding the lightning flashes down the sky, the Power that breathed in earthquakes and the bellowing of the storm, or sweetly sang his pleasure to them in the birds of spring and smiled his joy in the flowers by the road. Yea, out of this play must come a sustaining faith, their faith, a purified statement of aim and intent, of human purpose, or then all was waste and sacrifice made vain.

And so here on these yellow muted sands of Roanoke Island, let my hero, John Borden Everyman, speak out in the play on the night he and his companions are to disappear into the vast unknown out of our sight forever— let him speak the words which are his credo and our credo

as self-reliant and valiant men— "Hear that once Sir Walter
said, the victory lieth in the struggle, not the city won. To
all free men it standeth so, he said. And by the death of
our friends and companions and those who lie buried in
this ground, let us swear our consecration to the best that
is in us. Let the wilderness drive us forth as wanderers across
the earth, scatter our broken bones upon these sands, it
shall not kill the purpose that brought us here! And down
the centuries that wait ahead there'll be some whisper of
our name, some mention and devotion to the dream that
brought us here."

And let there be music, always music on which the story
might ride.

v

Thus I struggled with the drama, trying to make it say
something worthy of the lost and vanished people about
whom it was written.

Then as the months went by, the economic depression
settled on down in its deadening freeze of the nation's sap
and vitality. By this time hundreds of pledges had been
made, amounting to a total, I was told, of some two hundred
thousand dollars. But not one cent was ever collected from
these sources. Still, W. O. Saunders and his associate, D. B.
Fearing of Manteo, kept working, riding, talking, pro-
moting the idea of the drama, and even going to Washington to confer more than once with Senator Bailey, Congressman Warren and others.

Finally the agencies of the WPA, the CCC Camp, and
the Federal Theatre came into being. Through them and
with the cooperation of the North Carolina Historical Association, the Roanoke Island Historical Association, and
the Carolina Playmakers our project at last was realized.

An amphitheatre was built by the water's edge, costumes and lighting, chorus and actors provided, and with Samuel Seldon as director and Frederick H. Koch as advisory director, the play opened for its first annual summer run on the night of July 4, 1937—the first of the series of symphonic outdoor dramas.

Frederick H. Koch

Professor Koch believed that good teaching is the forming and guidance of students into the realization of their best latent possibilities. And he believed too that much of our modern teaching in schools, colleges and universities fails to bring out these possibilities—nay, too often stifles them and sends the student out into life distrustful, over-critical, uninspired and worst of all lacking a directive faith in himself, his fellows and the world around him.

Since the time of Darwin a hundred years or so ago, our western education has inclined more and more to be scientific, non-religious, non-inspirational and so-called practical, he said. The emphasis has been on things and facts and the behavior of things and facts. Our best brains and talents have busied themselves in seeking to understand material phenomena and the secrets of physical relationships and causes and effects. Our main effort has been to provide by cunning formulae and inventions a better manipulation and control of physical forces and projects and the making of gadgets for man's use and enjoyment—but for man as a natural, non-spiritual being, as an animal of the animal order if you will, who lives, loves, fights, kills, makes laws, breaks them, dies and presently returns a crumbling clod to the heart of the eyeless universe from which he sprang.

But however teasing and dramatic these challenges of nature and her materials were, Koch believed it was wrong to so urge the student to a confinement in and single devotion to them.

This sort of teaching, this sort of behavoristic philosophy, he felt, is by its very nature discouraging to the higher hopes and aspirations of human beings and must lead ultimately to despair, lead even to a world condition like the one which now prevails, where the best educated nations (best educated in a scientific sense, such as Germany, England, the United States) find themselves nerve-hung in an ironic situation of international antagonism from which there seems no way forward nor any way backward. For it is the nature of irony that no matter what action the protagonist takes, the result is mockery. And so in this stultification, a festering and decay will always set in and leadership and greatness go to inhabit elsewhere.

Well, yes, there is a way out and it lies in the direction of idealism, of a dedication to truth and the principles of a humane and civilized humanity—a man as a soul, a spiritual creative being, Koch said.

The engineer, the pragmatic scientist is only part of a man. The fulfilling part is the priest, the poet, the philosopher, and for Koch especially the artist. These come not first in time nor space nor condition necessarily but first in value and emphasis of concern. At least it seemed so to him.

He was not a scientist, was not a philosopher, but he instinctively had a sound grasp of the principles of true creative teaching. Apply his methods—if you can call them methods—to the training and guidance of young people, and these same young people would thrive abundantly, did thrive abundantly.

More than once I heard him say, "The longer I live the surer I am that what people need is not criticism but encouragement." And Proff—as we called him—did encourage people. He made them feel that they could do things, beautiful and noble things. His particular field was the drama, but his inspiration and idealism would have had the same significance in other fields. The categorizing, labelizing, marshalling of forces and influences to derive a poet forth, for instance, the cataloging and catechizing dear to the professional scholar, he felt were of small importance too compared to the experiencing of the wonder and glory of the subject at first hand.

"It is not the history of the flower," he said, "nor its name that is meaningful. In the deepest sense, it is the flower itself, the beautiful flower!"

Proff then was in the business of raising flowers, flowers of the imagination. His warm personality helped them to take root and thrive. And always the timid out-reaching tendril-twined student tended to unfold and grow in the sunlight of his favor.

His way of teaching was not popular with the scientific and scholarly professors at Chapel Hill. It couldn't be, no matter how much they might like him as a man. They considered his methods hit-or-miss. In fact he had no methods. His dislike for painstaking research or historical process offended their outlook and set of values. He was an enthusiast. And findings and contentions of enthusiasts are always in the final analysis—their phrase—likely to be unreliable. They found his graduate courses in English poor stuff, his playwriting class more like a group picnic than a meeting of serious workers. And as for his courses in Shakespeare, they were pretty farcical. He acted before his class. He read aloud. He recited. It was mostly Koch and little Shakespeare—so they said.

But the students would come away from his classes quoting *Romeo and Juliet*—

> "Look, love, what envious streaks
> Do lace the severing clouds in yonder east:
> Night's candles are burnt out, and jocund day
> Stands tiptoe on the misty mountain tops.
> I must be gone."—

or walk solemn and dewy-eyed under the spell of Ophelia's sweet and piteous suffering, murmuring to themselves—

> "White his shroud as the mountain snow,—
> Larded with sweet flowers;
> Which bewept to the grave did go
> With true-love showers."—

or mutter out in inner deep delight some of the mouthings of the monstrous and sullen Macbeth—

> "And all our yesterdays have lighted fools
> The way to dusty death. Out, out, brief candle!
> Life's but a walking shadow; a poor player,
> That struts and frets his hour upon the stage,
> And then is heard no more."

Proff made his students feel Shakespeare, he infected them, he inspired them with Shakespeare. Even when the message was mournful and despairing, the beauty of the poetry, the way he delivered it, were uplifting and thrilling.

He was an inspirer then, not a discourager. Despair was not in his heart, not in his world. He was creative, and his students felt this creativity and responded with their own.

This was good teaching, this was right teaching! It seemed so then and it still seems so to this student of his.

The Epic of Jamestown

(A Challenge to American Writers)

It was on the morning of April 26, 1607, just as dawn was breaking, that three tiny sailing ships, the Susan Constant, the Godspeed and the Discovery—none of them much larger than a modern liner's lifeboats—drew near the low Virginia coast. A lookout on the foremost ship suddenly cried out that land was sighted ahead, and the tidings were relayed to the other vessels. Cheers, prayers of thanksgiving, trumpet calls and beating of drums burst across the mist-shrouded water and up among the squealing seagulls already abroad for food.

Almost four months before, on New Year's Day, these colonists had left England bound on a hazardous voyage over a hazardous sea. Week after week, they had kept their faces westward—144 of them cramped in their unbelievably narrow quarters. And now they had reached their haven—the new land, Virginia.

They entered through the mouth of the Chesapeake Bay and went ashore. To their earth-starved senses, the country seemed a paradise. The air was balmy and filled with the odors of sweet shrubs and flowers, which they breathed in deliriously. All around were "fair meaddows and goodly Tall trees, with such Fresh-waters running through the woods," wrote one of them, "as I was almost ravished at the first sight thereof." They fell upon the earth, embraced it, clutched it to them, kissed it, and with streaming eyes gave thanks unto God, who had so mercifully preserved them from the perils of the deep.

They took possession of the land in the name of their sovereign, King James I, set up a cross, and named the place Cape Henry after the Prince of Wales. Then they set about looking for a site to build their settlement. Two weeks later they found what they wanted: a little island some fifty miles up the mighty Powhatan River (which they renamed the James), and far enough from the seacoast to give them protection from the big Spanish warships. Though the place was somewhat low and marshy—a fact which later would cost them heavily in sickness and death —the protection of the surrounding waters made it easy to defend. So there, on May 14, "Wee landed all our men."

England had made a number of attempts to plant settlements in North America before this, among them the expeditions headed by Sir Humphrey Gilbert, Bartholomew Gosnold and Sir Walter Raleigh. But all had failed. Raleigh had sent three successive groups of colonists to Roanoke Island, some hundred miles to the south. His last, with all its men, women and children, disappeared from the face of the earth and was never heard of again. After Raleigh, a number of forward-looking Englishmen had now taken up the bold business of colonizing. A private stock company, the London Company, was formed in 1605, and granted a charter by the King. These three ships were its first venture.

The stout resolution of those settlers who went ashore on Jamestown Island was equaled only by their ignorance of the difficulties ahead of them. Half of their number were gentlemen who had come, with their refiners, for the main purpose of discovering gold and silver for themselves and the company. The others were laborers, common soldiers, idle-footed fellows, a few carpenters, serving men and a sprinkling of boys.

The immediate need was to build a fort for protection against the antagonistic Indians. Land had to be cleared, too, and corn and vegetables planted at once, for the season was already far advanced. The strength of every man was needed to push the work ahead. So said Capt. John Smith, one of the bolder members of the governing council. He was for putting the gentlemen to work along with the others. At first this provoked a loud outcry. But finally necessity drove them to it.

Day after day, they swung their broadaxes, plied their whipsaws, hammers, shovels, trowels, mattocks and hoes—building their fort and their little rough-timbered wattle-and-daub cabins, cutting thatching reeds, digging ditches, clearing fields, sowing corn. The heavy embroidered capes, the plumed hats, the padded doublets, the fine Irish stockings of the gentlemen were soon laid aside, and so were the stout frieze jackets, the woolen hose and even the shoes of the common workers. They sweated and toiled as nearly naked as possible. The wilderness was already seasoning, and shaping them to its will.

Their store of meal, peas, oatmeal, oil, vinegar, salt and brandy began to run low. Much of it had spoiled on the long voyage. And the ships must now return to England for supplies. The finding of the gold mines would have to wait. A small show of sassafras, medicinal herbs, clapboards, cedar and walnut timbers to placate the waiting investors in London was loaded aboard, and Capt. Christopher Newport, the admiral of the fleet, sailed away, leaving 105 men behind.

The blinding heat of summer came down on the settlement in all its fury—such heat as few Englishmen had ever felt. And strange, loathsome diseases began to break out among them. The mosquito-ridden and malarial marshes had started taking their toll.

"There were never Englishmen left in a forreigne Countrey in such misery as wee were in this new discovered Virginia . . . If there were any conscience in men, it would make their harts to bleed to heare the pitiful murmurings and outcries of our sick men without relief every night and day for the space of six weekes, some departing out of the World, many times three or foure in a night; in the morning their bodies trailed out of their Cabines like Dogges to be buried."

Before the coming of autumn, more than half of the colony was dead. And to make matters worse, Captain John Smith, their most energetic leader, was ambushed by Indians and captured. Some of his men were slain, and he was taken to the old chief Powhatan to be killed.

Here occurred the famous John Smith-Pocahontas incident. As Smith was about to be executed, Pocahontas—"Powhatan's delight and darling, his daughter"—sprang between the prisoner and the descending clubs of the executioners and claimed his life as her own, a privilege that seems to have been allowed to any Indian, according to custom. Powhatan made Smith a member of the tribe, adopted him as his son, and concluded a peace between them, allowing Smith to return free to Jamestown. Because of this happening, the names of John Smith and Pocahontas have been linked romantically together in history and legend ever since. But there is not the least shadow of evidence for such romancing. Pocahontas was a mere child of twelve at the time, and the only Englishman she ever loved was John Rolfe, whom she met and married seven years later and by whom she had a son.

Captain Newport's return brought 120 new men and provisions, and also a strict injunction from the company that gold and silver must be found. A deposit of yellow earth was finally located back in the forest some distance from the fort, and the people went crazy with triumph. Spring was coming on again, and it was time to plant crops, but the half-mad settlers could think only of gold.

"There was no talke, no hope, nor work, but dig gold, wash gold, refine gold, load gold. Such a brute of gold, as one mad fellow desired to bee buried in the sandes, least they should by their art make gold of his bones." The ships were loaded with the stuff, and set off to England where it all turned out to be worthless dirt, ever to be described mockingly thereafter as "fool's gold."

Then came the winter of 1609-10 with its famous and terrible starving time. So fantastic and gruesome are some of the stories of that winter that but for the authenticity of the records one would be inclined to doubt their truth.

"Nay so great was our famine, that a Salvage we slew and buried, the poore sort took him up againe; and so did divers one another boyled and stewed with roots and herbs: And one amongst the rest did kill his wife, powdered her, and had eaten part of her before it was known . . . now whether she was better roasted, boyled or carbonado'd, I know not: but of such a dish as powdered wife I never heard of." The unfortunate and crazed murderer was chained to a stake and burned alive for his crime—"as hee well deserved."

Of more than 500 settlers who had reached Jamestown during these three first years, only sixty were alive when Sir Thomas Gates, the new governor, arrived in late May 1610.

His ship had been wrecked on the Bermudas ten months before, but the passengers and crew had been saved. And with two small ships constructed from the cedars on the islands he had made his way on to Jamestown.

Among the passengers was a quiet, devout young English farmer by the name of John Rolfe, who later, more than any other man, was to prove the savior of the colony. He brought with him some samples of Spanish tobacco seed and he immediately planted them. But before they could sprout, the decision was made to abandon the colony. For with the 150 hungry new mouths Gates had brought, starvation was certain if they remained.

On the morning of June 7, 1610, with their few pitiful belongings, they boarded their ships and sailed away from the scene of so much misery and woe. Jamestown was left deserted. But whether by good luck or divine intervention —and the devout John Rolfe certainly believed it was the latter—a timely meeting with Lord Delaware's supply ships in the mouth of the river saved the settlement.

By the winter of 1611, the company in England had had about enough. Not a glimpse of gold or silver had been found. No Indians had been converted to the true faith, no South Sea waterway to the riches of the Orient had been discovered. Nor had any exportable commodities been forthcoming. All efforts at making glass, soap, tar, pitch, pottery and iron to any commercial amount had failed. So had the experiments with silkworm culture and wine-making. For four years now there had been nothing but loss of money, ships and lives.

Still, there were a number of persevering souls in the London Company, like Sir Edwin Sandys, the Ferrar brothers, and Southampton, Shakespeare's friend and patron. One more, final, effort was decided upon.

Sir Thomas Dale was sent out as governor. A fierce, wide-walking soldier he was. He immediately took charge with an iron hand. Martial law was reaffirmed, and the death penalty invoked for all sorts of misdemeanors. It was death to speak against the King or the Governor. It was death to fail to attend church or to commit blasphemy, death to root up vegetables or destroy crops or slaughter cattle or to refuse to obey an officer's orders, no matter how trivial. It was death to trade a musket to an Indian, or to steal a chicken.

Until this time the colony had been living and working under a system of communism in which all earnings, provisions and supplies were put into a common storehouse. And however hard a man might labor or however energetic he might be, his share was the same as the worst laggard or malingerer. Rights and privileges that had been promised the settlers in the first charter, renewed in the second and reconfirmed in the third, had never been put into practice.

This communistic system, tried so unsuccessfully at Jamestown, antedated the Russian one by more than three hundred years, and the causes of its failure may still be valid. There simply was no incentive to individual initiative. Dale decided to change this. He allotted each man three acres of land to cultivate for his own use, conditioned on the paying of a tax of six bushels of corn annually into the public granary. Almost overnight the settlement was transformed into a body of more or less thrifty landed proprietors.

But the menace of the Indians continued. Unable to lead old Powhatan into any sort of decisive pitched battle by which he might break his power, Dale decided on another stratagem for peace. Learning that Pocahontas was visiting her relatives up in the Potomac region, he sent Captain Argall to kidnap her. This was accomplished by bribing her greedy old uncle, a petty chieftain, with a copper kettle to lure her aboard the captain's ship. She was brought back to Jamestown, and Dale sent word to her father Powhatan that he held her as a hostage and was now ready to talk peace and other matters. The old chief howled with grief over the capture of his daughter whom "he loved so dearly" but stubbornly refused to come to any terms.

For nearly a year, Pocahontas remained a prisoner at Jamestown, and during that time she was taught by John Rolfe and others "to speake such English as might bee well understood, [was] well instructed in Christianitie, and was become very formal and civill after our English manner." Pocahontas and Rolfe fell in love. She was baptized and christened Lady Rebecca, and on April 5, 1614, they were married there in the little church.

This marriage was one of the two definite reasons for the final permanence of the settlement. The other was tobacco.

Rolfe had been carrying on experiments with Spanish tobacco growing and was now curing a sweet and flavorsome product. Samples of it had already been sent to England where it had found immediate favor and a demand for more. Here at last, it seemed, was a commodity on which a stable export trade might be based and the future of the colony be the more assured.

The news of the marriage of Pocahontas to the hated white man was too much for Powhatan. He was old and tired now, and sick of the mutual slaughterings. The loss of his daughter was the last crushing blow. He agreed to a long peace with Dale and retired farther into the forest beyond the York River, there to live out his few remaining years in morose desolation.

With peace at last established, Dale began extending the settlement. And within two years a number of new centers were flourishing on the mainland—Henrico, Bermuda Hundred, Charles City, Martin's Hundred, and others. Dale felt his work was accomplished and he could now go home to the arms of the young wife he had left five years before. Though some 3,000 people had perished in the nine years of struggle, there were now 800 seasoned Englishmen in Virginia. The tobacco trade with the mother country was booming. The permanence of the settlement had become a certainty.

The mission of Jamestown's settlers at last had been fulfilled. The little hamlet remained the capital and political center of Virginia for some eighty years. During that time, a number of great events in the history of this country occurred there which should receive mention. The London Company had finally wrung from a reluctant King the rights and privileges that had so long been promised to the colony. And in the little Jamestown church on July 30, 1619, the chosen representatives of eleven hamlets and plantations met in the first legislative assembly in the New World "to make, ordain, and establish all manner of orders, laws, directives, instructions, forms and ceremonies of government and magistracy fit and necessary for and concerning the government of this colony."

A few days after this meeting, another event took place at Jamestown of tremendous significance to the future of this country. A Dutch ship landed twenty "Negars," who were sold to the planters to labor in the spreading tobacco fields. Thus, the birth of democratic freedom in the New World was all but coincident with the birth of slavery, its ironic twin.

In March, 1622, the worst Indian massacre on this continent struck the settlement. The colony now numbered more than 1,200, and Opecancanough, the chief, who succeeded Powhatan, determined to make one last desperate attempt to destroy his enemies and save his vanishing lands. With his warriors he fell upon the scattered hamlets and plantations and murdered 347 of the settlers before he was finally defeated and captured. But from then on the Indian power was broken. Thereafter the population grew rapidly.

The spirit of individualism and self-sufficiency increased, too, as the years passed. In 1676, the first armed struggle for liberty in America occurred at Jamestown. Angered by the tyranny of the Governor, Sir William Berkeley, and "oppressive navigation acts and high taxes," the citizens rose against the Governor, drove him to the mainland and burned the town. But young Nathaniel Bacon, leader of the rebellion, died at the height of his success and the movement collapsed.

The little capital was rebuilt, then in 1699 it was accidentally destroyed by fire again. The seat of government was then removed to Middle Plantation (later Williamsburg), and the island was pretty much abandoned.

At the end of the seventeenth century, the entire colony of Virginia numbered 80,000 people. The wilderness was fast being settled all along the coast, from Maine to Florida. A steady tide of migration was pushing up the rivers and bays, and far back into the interior to the mountains. In the splurge of growing and building and creating, the little hamlet was soon forgotten. Brambles and bushes grew up over the ancient landmarks and ruins. Later two or three resident tobacco farmers cleared some of these away, and their sharp-snouted ploughs passed over the graves of the forgotten dead.

In the year 1957 a reverent and grateful country turned again to this place of its beginning in a festival of commemoration. And the multitude of Americans who visited there for a moment did well for themselves if they remembered that the very soil beneath their feet was mixed with the mortal dust of thousands of men, women and children who perished there that a nation, our nation, might be born.

Three hundred and fifty years have gone by since those three little ships reached the shores of Virginia. And still for all that Jamestown has meant in our history, for all the suffering and heart-breaking endeavor and accomplishment there, no poet, composer, novelist or playwright in the long stretch of time has yet adequately told its story.

It cries out to be told.

Voice from Asia

"Yes," said the eloquent Asian philosopher with the
flashing eyes as we sat in his garden there in India, "I
admire the United States, your energy, your ability to get
things done. But most of all I admire your heritage, your
ideas. They are sound and good ideas. They are right, they
are true, like the ideas in your New Testament, in our own
religious epics. But unfortunately you too often have not
followed them—nor have we ours of course. But then we
are still a weak nation and the world is not looking to us
for guidance and much leadership as it is to yours. And
now this same world seems afraid that you are departing
from your ideas, losing them even. But I have faith you will
return to them, that you will not let them perish. In them
it seems to me lies much of the hope for the future. Humanity always looks to the future, you know. You are
now the most powerful country on earth and you have a
vast responsibility that goes with that power, but I wonder,
I often wonder, if your country realizes its responsibility
to the full. The world is looking to America for leadership,
but not leadership necessarily in physical power but leadership in terms of your democratic ideals, the ideals set down
by your Jefferson, Washington, Franklin, Adams, Madison,
Lincoln, Wilson, and others. And I think true leadership
can only come in terms of the vision such great men put
forth for the building of a nation—its thinking, its action,

its courage and beliefs. Many peoples in Europe, Asia, and now Africa, have been fired to aspirations of nationalism and freedom because of your own democratic philosophy of government. If you are to keep your leadership then you must make your democracy shine more brightly and not stay hid under a bushel of materialistic power.

"In the great gush of human activity, the splurge and turmoil of this modern age, the ideals that men live by, the moral and social visions which burn in their soul, the dreams that energize their minds and hearts, these are what will light humanity more brightly on its way. Your powerful western democracy is now being tested to the heart. And where once your pioneers were confronted with a vast physical wilderness, your present leaders through the means of our machine age of transportation and communication, of defense and attack, now are confronted with, even entangled in, a great wilderness of human and worldwide emotional and social relationships. But if in your national being there still lives the ideal, the vision, the dream if you will, of cooperation, of basic loyalty to truth and justice among men, and if you serve these principles, stand firm and do not fail them, then no matter what the storm and roar of perils and disasters raging about you, both you and the world shall the more surely weather these storms and go on toward universal peace, good will and prosperity among all men. I believe there is a moral bent, a way, a logos, in the nature of the universe and it is a moral one— the way of God, of Brahm. And without a firm foundation on it—in Him—all pragmatic accommodation, all displays and shows of physical power, all mighty aggrandizements of arms and territory, will ultimately perish and be as if they'd never been. And the bright and splendid gorge of youth, the gladsome servitors, will be shoveled to the boneyard of rot and oblivion as they would deserve to be.

"How fortunate you are in the United States to have to hand such a heritage of idealism, of moral integrity, to which you can keep turning for new understanding and inspiration and self-refreshment. The peoples in Europe and Asia and Africa know about it, it's in their school books, it's in the mouths of their teachers, on the lips of their leaders, sounded in the halls of their congresses and parliaments. And though it is sometimes hard to feel that these principles still live through the practices of your press, radio and television, and racial discrimination of your Southern politicians, still the people of the world feel it is there, and the turmoil of sex, guns and gangsterism spewed forth across the earth by your Hollywood motion pictures has not killed their belief in it.

"You not only have these ideals to sustain you in your leadership, but you have the story of how they were obtained, you have the full records of your early pioneers, your first settlers, their tremendous courage and endurance and their gradual self-sufficiency which eventuated in your doctrine of the equality of men and their rights to justice before the law and their opportunities and responsibilities as becomes free souls.

" 'The brilliant chariots of kings wear away, the body likewise waxes old, but the virtue of good people knows no age—' as it says in one of our books. 'And from bending in prayer one never grows crooked.' "

The Playwright in Revolt

The playwright, like other artists, is always in revolt, that is more or less. Not only is this true of artists, but likewise of people and things.

The word is a difficult one, and if a metaphysic for it were sought, it could be found in the old dualism of changing permanence stated in Greece some twenty-five hundred years ago and still a bafflement to the philosophers of this day.

It is the nature of that which exists—including the living and the dead—to make use of antagonisms and differences in the assertion of itself. In fact, such is the nature of that assertion.

Revolt then is but another term for development or growth—development which is contemporaneous in all existence, going on at any instant of time and in every part of space. In this sense all things are in continuous revolt, that is, all things are alive, with the constant qualification of more or less.

Thus any production is the production of something new from the old. Nor is this new ever the same as the old, for there can be no repetition either in nature, art or things, only similarity. In mechanisms where the methodology might demand sameness there is constant wear and tear and response to varying taste and needs and inner up-heavals. And there is no continuance in iteration.

The term development is more in keeping with a certain richer way of the world than revolt. The former means fulfillment of, and the latter denial of. And it would appear that life absorbs denial in its growth in so far as life is spiritual—if one may use a word so heavily suspect. And one must use it for completeness' sake, and in these latter days for the soul's sake.

II

Since the present, then, is always in revolt or developing, it is in that consequence the best of all possible times. It could not be otherwise, for in its development it contains the past, the present, and the future, inasmuch as they are significant to us the living: the past which has shaped us to the present, the past and the present upon which it feeds and acts, and the present and future which is its fruitfulness. And all are made one in action—action of men and things—which the philosophers describe as the process of becoming.

To repeat, this is truest of what might be called the spiritual nature of man and not of the process and wastage of physical nature and things. Accordingly the ancient statement that "now is the accepted time" is always true for man. Errors, mistakes, failures, and tragedies do not alter this, for negative and positive matters alike are one for him therein.

The recent preachment that the present is a time of cultural waste and decay has found widespread concurrence among the confused, the tired and discouraged who have been overpowered by the richness, variety, and upboilings of life and mistakenly apprehended these as antagonistic to art when in reality they are the food and inspiration of art.

Pessimism, therefore, is a partiality, and at any real moment of experience there is no cause for it. The weak keepers may tremble, but the light suffers no diminution, it ever increases. And Everyman ever grows stronger in his service to it. He neither revolts nor despairs, nor has ears for the phrases coming out of the distance that all is hopeless. These are ejaculations of hurt cast up in the heat of battle by the weak of arm and frail of will who fall afoul of themselves in the darkness near the edge of light.

And by that light Everyman writes in his book. He is the artist.

III

And as artist he is full of present great possibilities never before dreamed of and which he encompasses in his toiling and increasing wisdom.

With the canons of novelty and entertainment some would purvey him into their darkness, but confusion cannot dismay him nor can it deter him. For him beauty still walks upon the earth as in the days of any Naiad, Eve or Helen. Nor is the whole story told therein, for he will have his say and speak his vision, create his own testament of beauty.

And as artist he is stronger and freer in the living present. Like the rumor of old he increases by continuing, grows great by what he feeds upon. And his food is the multitudinous and ever-outpouring matter of life itself which fertile nature in all her forms provides.

And his spirit is freer than before in this province which is the all—the all that exists, all that can be thought or experienced. Nothing for him is tabooed or set apart or closed off. All is native to his need. All that is mechanical, all that

is vital with which the world is overflowing, all that has
been created—these are his.

IV

And as dramatist they are the inventions and the arts, the
facts and things and deeds and events of life, to be combined
and transformed with infinite variety into his dream made
manifest—history, poetry, music, painting, dancing, sculpture, architecture, pantomime: hills, streams, woods and all
weather, the sciences and all knowledge, and all the machinery of the modern world.

And from these he is creating the great art, the great
drama, which is his new religion, his new mystery and
philosophy.

V

And in the process his two ancient enemies fall before
him—diseased morality which would corrupt him, and commerce which would use him to its purpose, the former con-
fusing beauty with ethics and orthodoxy, the latter vision
with appetite and gain. The artist knows no immoral art,
no immoral drama. There can be bad art, bad drama. And
morality with its censorship must give way to aesthetic
taste and sensitivity, not to the enforcement of law.

For to consider fancifully, if art corrupts, it will corrupt
the judges of its corruption, and therefore the judges should
be protected, since if they are corrupted their judgment is
false and they are no longer judges and keepers of the truth
—and so on to absurdity. Law cannot in any way deal with
the matter, nor statute. Only intelligence and vision can.

And if art, the drama, to consider once more, is beholden
to gain, to commercial enterprises and rents, gambling and

exchanges, whims and fancies of its upholders, it is no longer art but a symbol of barter and vanity, in which beauty becomes a figment on an expedient currency.

All these things the artist knows and will show to others in time and as he can.

VI

And the dramatist writes the great drama for the theatre envisioned in this present. This theatre is the home of his art, with schools and training grounds, rooms, laboratories, and workshops for experiment in mechanics and all the arts —for all these will cooperate in the drama as it appears complete upon the stage of its new home, a home consisting of a studio, an auditorium, and an amphitheatre, these three being the reason for all other workshops and buildings begot around them.

And this home of buildings is the great theatre—with its director, its playwrights, its actors, artists, artisans, and inventors—all parts of the greater whole, to which they give existence and from which they draw inspiration.

And this too will suffer revolt and develop into something new and different. Such is the creative mystery and glory of both our art and our life.

A Visit to Hardy's Dorchester

(Some Random Travel Notes on Thomas Hardy **and**
His Town and His Interest in the Theatre)

I

Years ago on a hot summer night when I was a philosophy
student at Cornell University, I finished reading the tragic
story of *Jude the Obscure,* and from then on Thomas
Hardy its author was my man. I didn't change that opinion
with the reading of his other novels and his poems. Rather
my admiration for him increased, even right on through to
the last wrung grudging bit of optimism in *The Dynasts.*
I always hoped the time would come when I could get over
to England and meet him. Finally in 1928 the Guggenheim
Foundation gave me a ticket toward Europe to study the
drama and I set out. But malignancy was at work, as Hardy
himself would have wryly and maybe even impishly interpreted it, and I was denied the privilege of ever seeing him.
He died before I got there, and the strange and barbaric
English blood-rite of honor had already been perpetrated
upon him—his heart cut out and buried in Stinsford churchyard down in Wessex and the ashes of his body among the
great sleepers in Westminster Abbey.

After some months spent in Berlin, Paris and other European capitals, investigating the stage, seeing and reading

plays and meeting playwrights, I returned to London. Just
before I was to sail for home I saw a performance of
Hardy's *Tess of the D'Urbervilles*—a bad performance and
interminably long,—but even so it gave me a keen desire to
visit the Wessex country even in the short time left to me
and see some of the scenes which Hardy had made famous
in his descriptions, actions and characters. Though he himself was dead and gone, this at least would be something.

I arrived at Dorchester in the early afternoon of a hot
August day. I remembered that it was the anniversary of
the day years before when I had read *Jude the Obscure* at
Cornell. I was surprised at the smallness of the town. From
reading *The Mayor of Casterbridge* I had got the impression that it was much larger, a city in fact. It was a quiet,
ancient, sleepy place with some nine thousand inhabitants,
its streets narrow and winding. According to the guide
book, two Roman roads had once crossed here centuries
ago, one leading from Exeter eastward through Dorchester
up to Salisbury and on to London, the other from Weymouth on the coast through Dorchester and north to Il-
chester. The town was about seven miles from the sea, with
rolling country, grassy hills and meadows about, and a lot
of sheep-raising and dairying were in evidence. The prin-
cipal local industries, I found out, were an iron foundry
and the Dorchester brewery. Also a soldiers' barracks had
been placed here, which added to the local income and
social activity. In Roman times, Dorchester was called
Durnobaria, the guide book said, and was a center important enough to be enclosed with a wall. A fragment of the
wall still remains. In Saxon times it was known as Dorn-
ceaster or Dorecestre. Tradition has it that in 1003 King
Sweyn of Denmark captured and sacked the town and the
Normans rebuilt it. In 1613 it was almost completely destroyed by fire and restored again. Here Judge Jeffries held

his "Bloody Assize" in 1685, sentencing two hundred and ninety-two "rebels" to death and thus writing himself evilly down on the side of Hardyean darkness forevermore.

I got a taxi at the quaint old railroad station to a hotel, The King's Arms, where the Prince of Wales, later King George V, had once stayed, the proprietor told me, pridefully pointing out the silver service on display which the prince had used. But more interesting to me was the fact that in *The Mayor of Casterbridge* Michael Henchard once held a party here and the first Mrs. Henchard and her daughter Elizabeth Jane came at night and peeped through the windows to see the splendid goings-on within. By these windows and by this door more than one Hardy character had passed on his way to a tragic doom the author had prepared for him. I got a room for six shillings and while waiting for lunch to be made ready went out to buy a shirt. Two doors up the street a sign proclaimed one Jackman as "clothier." I went in and bought my shirt and in the process I asked Mr. Jackman casually about the town.

"American, are you?"

"Yes."

"Several of 'em come here now and then. So you're interested in the town?"

"Yes I am."

"There's plenty to be interested in around here. History —more history than a man knows what to do with. Come here. Let me show you." He took me to the back of the store, opened the door and pointed across the little refuse-littered back square. "Right there," he said, "is where the old Roman Road ran, one of 'em did. You can see pieces of flint and rock there that made the bed on which the war chariots rumbled by." Then we turned back into the store. "See that post there?" And he indicated an upright in the middle of the floor which supported a huge sagging beam overhead. "Well, when we were digging down in the ground here to put up that post we scraped out all sorts of things. Ah, the people that have lived here and been buried in this ground!" He stared off a moment, considering the fact.

And there echoed across my mind something of what Hardy had said in *The Mayor of Casterbridge* concerning Susan Henchard's burial in the nearby churchyard—where her dust mingled with the dust of ancient women who lay there ornamented with glass hairpins and amber necklaces, and men who held in their mouths coins of Hadrian, Posthumus, and the Constantines.

"What sort of things did you dig up?" I finally asked.

"Oh, old pots and pitchers and pieces of vases and jugs and a few fidos. I've got some of the stuff in a sack back there. I'd be glad to give you some of it if you want it."

"I certainly would."

"You come back after your lunch then and I'll haul it out. I'm busy just now."

He tied up the shirt, handed it to me and I paid him. While he was getting change from the cash drawer I asked him if he had known Thomas Hardy, the writer, who used to live here.

"I did. He's dead now," he said. "I knew him well— queer man in a way, and not so queer either. But you had to know him to know how to take him."

"Yes."

"I don't mean he was too peculiar, but he never had much to do with anybody. He'd come into town—he lived some distance out—he'd come in here and do his trading and then go back to Max Gate out there a mile or two where he lived. He'd always walk or ride a bicycle till he got too old. Then sometimes he'd come in a carriage. He'd never talk much, at least I never heard him." A customer came into the shop then and he nodded to a clerk who had been listening. The clerk went off to wait on the customer, and Mr. Jackman continued. "Yes, everybody knew Mr. Hardy."

"You used to put on plays of his here in the town, didn't you?"

"We did, a lot of them. And that's when I saw most of him. I acted in some of the plays myself."

"You called your group the Hardy Players, didn't you? That's what I've heard."

"Yes, that was the name we got to be called by, though at first we were a literary and debating society. Still long ago we used to do a few dramatic things on the side too. Come out this way again." He took me to the rear door once more and pointed to a low building across the little square at the back. "See that building? That's the Corn Exchange. That's where we did the plays. Many's the time I've acted on that stage in there. It stays locked up most of the time. It's not much of a place to look at. Seats and a stage, that's about all."

"And a curtain?"

"Yes, we had a curtain, and lights too. But of course not like they have it up in London. But we had a lot of fun, a lot of fun and trouble too."

"Don't you put on plays any more?"

"Hardly any more. So many other things have come up. And then the war got everything disrupted. And Mr. Hardy's dead. No, we're not active the way we once were." In a sort of stable at the right a dog began a loud and sudden howl. Mr. Jackman shouted out at him, "Hush your fuss, hush, I tell you!" Then he turned back to me. "My dog broke his leg a month ago and has to be chained up. He gets impatient all right. Yes, well you come back after lunch and I'll get some of that pottery stuff out and show you."

"I'll appreciate it."

I went off to the hotel and put on my clean shirt. After lunch I returned to the store.

"Well, here you are," Mr. Jackman said. He hauled out a small cardboard box from under the counter and showed me two or three dozen pieces of broken ware. We looked it over and I tried to conceal my disappointment. He seemed to sense it and spoke up quickly. "Of course we put the best stuff in the museum over there. A lot of things we put in there—amongst 'em a fine vase. You can see it. It's said to be the best collection of antiquities 'most anywhere except maybe up in London." He jiggled the broken bits rapidly in his hand, and then held up the tops of two narrow-necked jugs or vases. "Would you like these?" he asked.

"Yes, if you can spare them."

"Now I come to think of it, I'm afraid I can't. They're nothing but door knobs, but my little daughter wants 'em. I remember I promised 'em to her." He took up the jagged-edged bottom of a vase. "You can have that, if you want it," he said.

"That'll be fine. Thanks very much."

We talked for a while about the industries of Dorchester, the surrounding country, some of its ancient landmarks and history. But he seemed to have read the guide book no better than I, and guide book information was about all he gave me.

"Is there a bookstore in town?" I finally asked.

"Yes, there is. No doubt you'll be wanting to get some of Mr. Hardy's books."

"Yes, I may. Are any of the plays published?"

"Plays?"

"I mean those the Hardy Players used to give in the Corn

Exchange. I looked around in London but couldn't find any."

"Oh no, I don't think so. We always had 'em copied out —our parts, I mean. Mr. Tilley and Mr. Evans used to make plays from Mr. Hardy's novels. That's what we acted mostly, Mr. Hardy's stuff. That's why we were called the Hardy Players maybe. Yes, there's a bookstore. Right across the street there, run by a man named Ling. It sounds Chinese but it's good English. He knows a lot about Mr. Hardy, more than I do. In fact he used to publish some of Mr. Hardy's poems and things, but no plays. You ask him. He'll tell you."

"By the way, you spoke of digging up some 'fidos'," I said.

He broke into a laugh. "Yes. I mean dog bones. We've dug up lots of them. The Romans must have loved dogs and had plenty of 'em around. We throw most of the bones away. Here's a piece of one." And he lifted a little black crumbly object between his fingers. "You can have it if you want to, but it'll fall all to pieces in your hand if you're not careful."

"Thanks."

I wrapped up the bone and the little vase fragment in a piece of paper and went out and across the street to the stationery and book store. The windows of the store were full of Hardy's books and books on Hardy and Wessex. This was honor in one's own country and neighborhood and I felt glad. As I went into the store two or three girl clerks were standing about waiting for customers, customers who seemed to be rare in all the Dorchester stores, though it was Saturday afternoon.

"Can I do something for you?" one of them asked. And all three came forward.

"I was looking around for something to read."

"Something on Mr. Hardy?" the tallest girl said, and she cut a faint smile backward and around to the other two girls. "We've got a few rare first editions."

"No, I might get something cheap to read. I'll just look about if you don't mind."

"Please do."

There were illustrated books on the Hardy country, all kinds of postcards giving views of Hardy landmarks and even Hardy calendars. Finally I bought a small edition of Hermann Lea's excellent *Highways & Byways in Hardy's Wessex*, for six shillings. I had borrowed it from the university library back home once and read it. As the tall girl was wrapping it up, I asked her if she had known Mr. Hardy.

"No, I didn't know him. I'm new here. But Mr. Ling did. He knew him well. I've heard him talk about him."

"I was told Mr. Ling published some of Mr. Hardy's books."

"No, I don't think so. He published the programs for the Hardy Players but that's about all, I think."

"Have you any programs left?"

"I think so. I'll see. We keep most of them locked in the safe. They're very rare, you know." Again she gave that faint smile at one of the other girls and went into a little boxed-up office at the rear of the room. Presently a red-faced youngish man of thirty or more wearing gold-rimmed spectacles came out. He had his hand in his wide coat pocket, and his look was all business.

"Good day, sir," he said. "Yes, I have just a few programs left." He pulled a number out of his pocket carefully. "They are scarce, rare, and getting scarcer. You know the Hardy Players are not active as once they were."

"Yes, I know."

"It's a privilege to own one of these."

"I'm not interested in collecting, so—"

"Let me show you. We did all of Mr. Hardy's local printing. Here for instance is a program of the first production of *Tess*. The only one I have, but I would let it go."

"How much is it?"

"Eh! Oh, naturally it's expensive. They are snapped up fast as anything. The last one I sold, I remember, was to another American. He paid me two guineas for it. He came from Ohio or somewhere. I forget his name. But he was glad to get it. Still, I'll let you have this one. It's a bargain, the same price—two guineas."

"Well, I'm afraid I can't buy it then. And what are these worth?" I asked, and I turned through theatre programs of *The Return of the Native*, *The Queen of Cornwall*, *Desperate Remedies*, *The Trumpet Major* and *The Three Wayfarers* which for some reason were lying loose on a table close by.

"They are rare, too, but I suppose in a pinch I could let you have them at a guinea each."

I laid them regretfully down. He reached again into his pocket and pulled out a little pamphlet. "Here is a short poem of Mr. Hardy's. He had the custom of sometimes sending me a single poem and having it printed and bound like this. Then he'd pass copies around to his friends on birthdays and Christmas time, you know. This is a proof copy. There's only one mistake in it. If I'd a-known he was going to die when he did I would have seen to it there were lots of mistakes for him to correct. It would have made it more valuable, you know. No, I don't suppose I could sell that for any price. He gave it to me. I remember the day he was in here. He looked at me in the face with that quiet way of his and said, 'You're welcome to it.'" He put it back into his pocket abruptly and quickly. "No, he gave it to me. I'd best not sell it." Going to his little box-office, he returned immediately with three volumes of *The Dynasts*. "The first volume of this is a second, the other two are firsts," he said. "You can have the three of them for fifteen pounds. If it was complete, it would be worth three hundred."

"Oh, but that's a small fortune."

"But up in London they are paying fortunes for Hardy books. His first editions are bringing pounds, pounds."

"At Foyle's the other day I—"

"I don't know him," he said sharply.

"He's the largest book dealer in London. In his store I was offered a copy of *Jude*, first edition, for two pounds. There were others as cheap. I remember *Life's Little Ironies*."

"Then you'd better bought 'em," he said.

"Maybe so," I said.

"You could a-made money on 'em."

"Maybe," I said.

"Well, how about one of these programs?"

"No, I don't believe so—not today, thank you."

"No, I guess you're not a collector," he said a little resignedly.

"I'm not. I'm just down here to visit the countryside in which Mr. Hardy lived and to talk to some of his neighbors about him."

"Many people come here that are interested in Mr. Hardy," he said. And then he smiled, and his smile was nice and friendly. "And they buy books too."

"Mr. Jackman tells me you knew Mr. Hardy well."

"Oh no, not me. I knew him, but not too well. He must have been talking about Mr. Ling. I'm not Mr. Ling. I've been here only a few years. Now Mr. Ling knew him from —oh, years and years. Pity he's not in now. He's away on business. He'd be glad to talk to you. He loves to talk to people about Mr. Hardy. And the things he knows—the anecdotes, the stories, the little incidents, his association with Mr. Hardy. Still, I know a good deal about him too, somewhat from hearsay and from casual acquaintance, if you know what I mean. Are you writing a book on Hardy?"

"No, I've liked his work a long time, and having the chance, I thought I'd come down here for a day or two and look around."

"Yes, do that. Enjoy yourself while you're here. You'll be able to see a lot. This is an old, old town as you no doubt have already found out. There's a great deal of history attached to it." And then he laughed and winked. "Sometimes I think that's what's the trouble with it—too much history. The past pulls it down. It can't get loose, wake up and boom along the way your American cities do." And he sighed and looked off. "Yes, it's got a deal of history. But that don't keep it from being dull—at times. As I said, maybe that's why it's dull. I've thought of going out to America, or Spain maybe." And he gazed through the door and far, far away. "A lot of my friends have left here and gone out in the world. The young people leave here. The old stay. Of course Mr. Hardy loved it. He wouldn't have been satisfied to live anywhere else. It suited him. But then he was a writer, an artist, and I'm not."

"I thought I would see some of the places he wrote about."

"Yes, you do that. It would be interesting. Of course Mr. Hardy changed the names of nearly all the towns and streets and the like. He made up a number of new names of places, characters too. But anybody acquainted with the country can spot most nearly every one of them."

"Yes, like Mr. Lea here in his book. I've just bought it."

"That's a good book, I read it."

"You said a moment ago you knew Mr. Hardy—casually, in passing."

"Yes, I knew him. And in a way I might say I knew him pretty well, but of course not like Mr. Ling. He was rather hard to get to know, Mr. Hardy was. But you could learn how to take him. He used to come into the store here. And I'd let him alone. He would look at the books quietly and maybe finally buy one, though I must say he hardly ever did buy anything. Most people thought he was sort of stingy and stand-away. Maybe he was. But he was a kind man and not queer at all when you got to know him."

I waited for him to go on, but he picked up a duster and began brushing among the cards and books as if finished with me.

"Can you tell me where he's buried? I'd like to go to his grave."

His duster stopped in mid air. "Hah," he said. Then lowering the duster, he cocked his head at me. "Part of him's buried right down the road there in Stinsford Churchyard and the rest is buried up in Westminster Abbey." He looked at the floor a moment, laid down his duster and wiped his spectacles. "Wasn't that a queer way to treat a man?" Adjusting his spectacles, he went on. "Mr. Hardy left it in his will that he was to be buried in the graveyard there by his first wife, and then they did him like that. Shameful, I think it was."

"Perhaps it was."

"No perhaps about it. Looks like the dead might have their wishes listened to. And he would have, if it hadn't been for that man Barrie."

"Sir James Barrie?"

"Yes, him."

"What did he do?"

"There was a lot of talk among the literary folks about where to bury Mr. Hardy. Telegrams and letters poured in here. But Mrs. Hardy said she would stick by the will, and so it was. And preparations were being made. Then here come Mr. Barrie all hot down from London and persuaded her to have his body—his ashes—buried in Westminster. They were great friends, you know, Mr. Barrie and Mr. Hardy, and Mr. Barrie wanted him to have that honor. 'So few writers,' he said, 'are worthy of it. But Mr. Hardy is worthy,' he said. And finally he persuaded Mrs. Hardy to do it. But why couldn't they have buried him here in Stinsford the way he wanted, and then put up a tablet to him there in Westminster? I ask you that?"

"It seems they could have."

"They could. Think of them cutting and sawing into him the way they did. Taking out his heart! Aye, a tablet would have done just as well—to my way of thinking better."

Here a customer came in and stood waiting. He turned away and called out as he left, "Plenty of people in Dorchester think it was a shame too, just the way I do."

I waited a while but he didn't come back.

Mr. Jackman was standing in the door of his store as I came out into the street and called out to me, "If you're interested in Thomas Hardy and his plays, you ought to see Mrs. Major—Mrs. Ethel Major. She runs a cafe and tea room right up there near the corner of Cornhill street."

I thanked him and went on. An old church attracted my attention off at the right, and I turned down that way. Passing along the front of the building, I entered the churchyard. Slab after slab lay all around me lichened over, with the carved names of the dead on them almost worn away and in some cases completely obliterated. Everywhere about me I could feel the spirit of Hardy—in the moss-grown graves, the overhanging trees, the mournful dark shrubbery and the crumbling old native stone of the church itself—the spirit of Thomas Hardy's brooding rebellious genius. The crying of a child broke in upon my thoughts and off at the left standing by an ancient grave, I saw a weeping little boy. He had made a mess in his trousers—a tragedy equal to any of Hardy's for him. His mother was pulling up bunches of grass and trying shame-facedly to clean him off. When he saw me his wailing became louder. Unwilling to add to his sufferings by my presence, I went away.

On the street again I asked a passerby what church this was. "Saint Peter's," he said. And I remembered that it had figured in *The Mayor of Casterbridge* and other stories. I went on up the street to Mrs. Major's cafe. She was a frank bustling woman of some forty-five or fifty, with an intelligent genial face. Her eyes lighted up when I told her I wanted to talk to her about Thomas Hardy and especially about his interest in the theatre.

"Yes," she said. "I'm glad to talk with anybody about Mr. Hardy," and she made an untying motion toward the knot of apron behind her. But she bethought herself and dropped her hands. "I can't leave my work just now," she said, "but if I could I'd take you home and show you the great bundles of clippings and notes and things I've got."

"Maybe I could see them later," I said.

"Yes, you may," she replied. "You come back at six thirty and I'll have it all laid out for you." Then she told me how to find her place.

II

I walked down Cornhill and South streets out to the Roman amphitheatre where gladitorial combats and battles between men and wild beasts were supposed to have been held in the long ago by the Roman conquerors. This place is mentioned several times in Hardy's stories and novels. Its elliptical shape was still clearly visible with its banked incline on either side where once seats had been built for spectators. I remembered that Lea in his book had said it was one of the finest, if not the finest, of Roman amphitheatres remaining in all Britain. I asked a passing constable how I could find my way to Maiden Castle, another Hardy landmark. In ancient times it was Mai-Dun,—said to be a stronghold of Ptolemy—and thus in later language Maiden—"of huge dimensions and many ramparts."

"It's over there," he said, pointing far across a field toward a long looming hill that stretched against the sky. I thanked him and set out. The field had recently been reaped, and rows and rows of oat stacks were set like a multitude of great bee-hives symmetrically around. Evidently the land was rich. The crop was good. Off to the left were two silent and waiting reaping machines. A stiff gale was blowing, but I stuck my head down and pushed on into it toward this high hill of prehistoric defense in the distance. I finally reached a fence and passed on through a wooden gate. A flock of sheep marked and smeared with reddle followed bleating and friendly after me, and I was reminded of the long-suffering Diggory Venn, the reddle-man, in *The Return of the Native*. I reached a second fence and gate at the base of the hill and went through, leaving the sheep behind. I mounted up over ditch and ridge and ditch again and finally to the level top. Here and there were patches and holes dug as if huge gophers or some of Hardy's antiquarians had been recently at work. On top of the earth ramparts was a shepherd's hut wagon. For an hour I explored the winding turns, the time-clogged furrows and trenches, imagining to myself the ancient embattled people who had stood and fought and died here. In a half-nature piece and story entitled "A Tryst at an Ancient Earthwork" Hardy described this "stupendous ruin" as only Hardy could—a piece of writing, I think, the equal of his famous picturing of Egdon Heath at the beginning of *The Return of the Native*. I remembered too that it was here that Michael Henchard in *The Mayor of Casterbridge* used to watch for Elizabeth Jane as she took her walks on the Budmouth Road. To think that that ancient race of men, thousands of years before the Romans, were able with reindeer horn, picks and stone axes and mauls to create such a defensive stronghold! And then the Romans themselves! What pride, what strut of their conquerors' power had walked here—these too to yield to stilling time—and the swallowing earth!

Cutting up clean against the sky off to the west was the monument to Admiral Hardy, one of the collateral line of Hardys and a hero in the battle of Trafalgar. There on that upland, tradition had it, signal fires were lighted in the hours when Napoleon was expected to invade England in the early 19th century. Hardy speaks of this in one of his short stories, "A Tradition of Eighteen Hundred and Four" and also in *The Dynasts*.

Late in the afternoon I returned across the fields to the town and to Mrs. Major's for tea. She showed me a miscellaneous bundle of Hardy material which she had brought out and placed on the table.

"It's all mixed up," she said apologetically. "I just love to get things together and I do it without much system or order."

"That's the best way to collect things," I replied, eyeing the package hungrily.

"You won't have time to look at it all now," she said. "Have some more tea and then you can take the pile to the hotel and look through it tonight."

"Thank you," I answered heartily. "You trust me with it?"

"Of course. You'll bring it all back."

"Every piece of it," I said. And then we sat chatting for a while, and she talked glibly and authoritatively about the Hardy country.

"Would you like to go see his birthplace?" she asked.

"Yes, I would."

"It's not very far," she said, "but too far to walk as late as it is today. Perhaps tomorrow."

"Maybe we could get a taxi and go now," I prompted.

"Yes, let's do that," she said jumping up.

We went down to The King's Arms, found a taxi and set out. We passed by the little Three Mariners' Hotel where Michael Henchard and Elizabeth Jane had put up in the days gone by, they not having the price of the more expensive hotels. Then we went by the White Hart, a few doors further down, which figures in many of Hardy's stories and from which the van used to set out for Long Puddle and other places so vividly described in Hardy's volume, *Life's Little Ironies.*

"There used to be a market square in front of the White Hart," said Mrs. Major, "and Mr. Hardy tells of it in a number of his tales and novels."

A few yards farther down at the foot of the town was a little bridge. "See this bridge," said Mrs. Major, "where the heels of generations of loafers sitting on the stone railing have knocked great troughs out of the bricks underneath. More respectable loafers used to sit on Grey's Bridge which is ahead of us there and not so easy to be seen from the town. This bridge here is called Swan's Bridge, and it was here that Sergeant Troy used to wait for poor Fanny Robins in the book, *The Trumpet Major.*"

"Yes," I murmured.

Two hundred yards or so farther we crossed Grey's Bridge and Mrs. Major pointed out the warning of "transporting" engraved thereon against malefactors. "Grey's Bridge is famous in Mr. Hardy's books," she said. "In *The Mayor of Casterbridge*, in *The Trumpet Major* and it's also mentioned near the end of *Under the Greenwood Tree*. Dick Dewy and Fancy Day used to walk this way, and the lovelorn vicar too. Mr. Lea tells about it in his book. See that path there across the meadow. Many a Hardy youth and maid have walked that path," she said pensively. "Just over there is Stinsford Church. Mellstock it is called by Mr. Hardy," she went on. "You remember the Mellstock Choir."

"I do that," I answered.

"We might stop in there for a minute though it's getting late. You ought to come back tomorrow and see it."

After about a mile's driving we turned in at the church for a moment, just long enough to see the muffled tombstones of the Hardy family off in the shadows there and to have an outside look at the quaint old church. Then we drove on toward the Hardy birthplace some three miles distant. We arrived there just before twilight. Mrs. Major introduced me to the lady of the house, a Mrs. Pouncy—a name that might have come right out of *Under the Greenwood Tree*. She was at supper but seemed glad to see us and showed us over the house. The building was a long thatched cottage two stories high and a single room in depth. She took us up the creaky stairway to Thomas Hardy's little room. A small boy was asleep in the bed—her nephew she said, so we talked in whispers. "People come here," said Mrs. Pouncy, "and I'm always glad to show them about. You see this window here which looks down on the little garden. Mr. Hardy wrote three of his novels here. Let me see—*Desperate Remedies*, *Under the Greenwood Tree*, and

Far from the Madding Crowd. He wrote them right by that window sitting on a sugar box. Mrs. Hardy has the box at Max Gate now. Sir James Barrie comes down here often. He was here not long ago and he just stands and stands, looking out of that window down into the garden. I wonder what's on his mind. Many a time I've felt like asking him. But I daren't. And he just looks and says never a word."

Then she took us downstairs and into another room and pointed to the fireplace. "Right there by that fireplace is where Thomas Hardy got his inspiration. There night after night his mother Jemima used to sit telling her stories to young Thomas. A wonderful woman she was—a great reader, too, and knew a lot in books. And she could do anything with her hands—sew, cook—anything. She lived to be old, past ninety when she died. Mr. Hardy worshipped her and used always to put flowers on her grave. Yes, that's the way it is, a mother's influence can make or break a man. It made him."

"And where is Egdon Heath?" I finally asked.

"Right out there," she said pointing. "It comes almost down to the house. A lonely place it is. Yes, maybe that heath had something to do with Thomas Hardy's imagination too. Come outside," she said, "and maybe you can see the heath through the trees. But wait a minute. I've got some postcards here. Maybe you'd like to buy some."

I bought a number and then we went outside. It was dark but I thought I could see the heath shouldering itself up beyond the trees.

After we left, we turned and drove down a lane, a lane which, Mrs. Major explained, Thomas Hardy had walked many a time as a boy on his way to school. "And Mr. Hardy walked it many times after he got to be a grown man," she said, "communing with himself." We drove on in silence for a while. Finally Mrs. Major said, "We are passing through lower Mellstock now where Fancy Day taught school. There on the right you can see the Greenwood Tree." We stopped the taxi and looked at it for a moment, a rich overflowing mass in the darkness.

"Is it a beech?" I asked. "I don't remember."

"Yes, that's what it is, a beech," she said. "On this way back to town we will pass Max Gate, his home. Would you like to stop there?"

"Yes, I would," I said. Presently the taxi pulled up by the side of the road. I got out, opened the wide swinging gate and walked up the path.

A big ungainly brick house, as well as I could make out, loomed up in the vague darkness. No light was visible anywhere. It looked so lonely and forlorn that I stopped and gazed at it for a moment. I turned and went back to the taxi.

"You didn't go in?" said Mrs. Major.

"No," I answered lamely, "perhaps tomorrow. There doesn't seem to be anybody at home."

"Oh, yes, Mrs. Hardy's at home. She's always there except when she's in London. I know she's there now. You needn't have minded. She's very kind and understanding."

"Then I'll come tomorrow," I said.

We drove on back to town and to the King's Arms. Mrs. Major had supper with me and afterwards we went into the lounge and I made some notes of the things she told me.

"The first Mrs. Hardy was 'county folks,' " she said. "Like Mr. Hardy she loved the outdoors. They used to ride bicycles a lot, also walk. Mrs. Hardy—I've seen her many and many a time—used always to ride her pale green bicycle wearing a dark green velvet frock. She was always very dressy. She also liked to ride horseback. Mr. Hardy was completely devoted to her, I know. He was of humble birth and she higher, but he loved her no matter what the hints were. She was a beautiful woman. They loved the outdoors in common, always walking or riding together.

"They were both devoted to animals too. Mr. Hardy had a dog named Wessex, a rough-haired terrier, and he was very sad about its death. He designed a tombstone for it and buried it in the garden at Max Gate, and also wrote a poem for it—about it. After Wessex and others of their pets had died, Mr. Hardy said they'd not have any more. Their dying was too sad, he said. 'It's better for a man not to have any pets' he said. But he did have a few others.

"He and Colonel Lawrence of Arabia were close friends. I remember when we gave *Tess* at Weymouth he went down, though he was eighty-four, with Colonel Lawrence. They both stayed till late in the night and drove back home. Mr. Hardy used to come to every performance of *Tess* here in Dorchester. He'd come and take his seat and never say anything. He was much attracted to Gertrude Bugler's acting of the part. Yes, he was always deeply interested in the stage and wanted to write plays too. He made a number of dramatizations of his own stories. They weren't as good as the originals though—at least I don't think so."

"Which of his stories and novels did he dramatize himself, Mrs. Major?"

"Well, he wrote *The Queen of Cornwall* as a play to start with—one-act you know—in Shakespeare verse."

"Yes, I've read it."

"He made a one-act piece out of *The Three Wayfarers* back in 1893. But we didn't produce it here till 1911. He made a play out of *The Return of the Native*. Mr. Tilley did too, and his was better than Mr. Hardy's, and we produced that back in 1920. He dramatized *Tess* in 1894–5— two versions and laid them aside for nearly thirty years. It was 1923 before we put it on, the second version. Yes, he was always interested in playwriting. I've often heard him say he wished he could write plays. I don't remember that he made any more dramatizations. If he had I'm sure I would have known about it. Of course he helped Mr. Evans and Mr. Tilley in their dramatizations—that is, he conferred with them when they came for help and advice. They did most of our Hardy scripts."

"What novels and stories did they make into plays?"

"Let me see. Back in 1908 they did *The Trumpet Major*. Then in 1909 *Far From the Madding Crowd*. A year or so later *The Mellstock Quire*—that was the name we gave to the play from *Under the Greenwood Tree*—the original title Mr. Hardy had for the novel itself. And next it was *The Distracted Preacher* and *The Woodlanders*. And then there were *Wessex Scenes* from *The Dynasts*, *The Return of the Native*, as I say, and *A Desperate Remedy*. I remember them so well because I played in about all of them."

"What parts did you play, Mrs. Major?"

She laughed and went on. "Mind you I'm no actress, but I did enjoy it, and I miss it now we've stopped. Well, I played—let me see—Matilda Johnson in *The Trumpet Major*, Mrs. Penny and Mrs. Dewey in *The Mellstock Quire*, The Shepherd's wife in *The Three Wayfarers*, Mrs. Simpkins in *The Distracted Preacher*, Mrs. Crickett in *A Desperate Remedy*, Mrs. Yeobright in *The Return of the Native*, a Shade in *The Queen of Cornwall*, and Mrs. Durbeyfield in *Tess*."

"That must have been a wonderful experience, playing all those parts," I spoke up enthusiastically.

"Yes, it was wonderful," she said, "and I learned a lot. Mr. Ridgeway came down here from London to get me to play Mrs. Durbeyfield in the production there. But I was gone to London myself that day and so missed him. But I couldn't have gone to act in it. I have my business to attend to here."

She stared off an instant in silence, then shook her head as if dismissing some bothering thought. "But to go back to Mr. Hardy's love of animals and living things.

"One night two entomologist friends of his were out in the field near his house catching moths along the hedges with a net. It was about one o'clock in the morning, and he was up working—maybe writing at his poems, for he'd stopped writing fiction. Presently they heard a voice behind them. 'You shouldn't be trying to trap these animals. Don't you know that?' It was Mr. Hardy. He'd seen their light from his study window upstairs and thought they were poachers. He hated any sort of cruelty to animals or anything. No man had a kinder and softer heart.

"Mr. Hardy was awfully clever at anything he did—drawing, painting, music, anything. Once when we were rehearsing *The Mellstock Quire* at Christmas and couldn't get some of the music right, he took the fiddle and played the tunes through and then showed us the dances. He cut the steps himself though he was an old man then. He used to show us all the dances and music in the plays and help us at rehearsals. His father and grandfather were musicians, fiddlers, before him, and he was as you might say raised on music. He and his father used to play at dances and randies, he a little boy even going along and playing second fiddle to his father's first. And they played many a year at services in Stinsford Church too. Yes, Mr. Hardy was wonderful at remembering old tunes and steps. He never got it wrong.

"His mind was unimpaired to the last. There didn't seem to be much wrong with him, but he was so old and tired. I don't think he wanted to live. He had seen so much, thought so much and worked so hard. Yes, he was just tired, I'm sure.

"The second Mrs. Hardy was very devoted to him. He would never have lived as long as he did if she hadn't protected him from everything. He was very sensitive, and in his old days the least little thing would upset him. She was his secretary for a long time before she married him.

"Mr. Hardy was strangely susceptible to women. A pretty woman would take his attention to the last. He wasn't so much interested in our production of *Tess* perhaps as he was in Mrs. Bugler in the part. He used to come all the time to rehearsals and performances at the Corn Exchange and sit and watch her act. I've heard him say she looked like Tess to him. I don't mean he—er—loved her. No. He just loved to look at her.

"He used to say he hoped her acting the part wouldn't get her too much interested in the stage. He was afraid of what that might do to her life. She was a Bugler and married to a Bugler—same name though no kin so far as I know —a butcher. Now she's up in London playing the part. All of us wonder what will happen to her. She is a most extraordinary woman and seems to live the very part of Tess. Not interested in any other part, although she has played other Hardy parts in the plays here. In her way she too is a genius."

I promised Mrs. Major to return her bundle of material the next morning and so we said goodnight. For the next hour or two I sat in my room in the hotel making notes— among them this from *The Dorset County Chronicle* of November 26, 1908:

"Never was such a thing witnessed in a Dorchester playhouse as on Wednesday night when there were to be observed in the front seats a posse of leading dramatic critics who had come from London especially for the occasion, and the telegraph messenger stood at the front exit ready to dart off to the telegraph office with critiques, etc. It was of course an act of homage paid to the author of the Wessex novels and creator of *The Wessex Romance*.

"It was indeed interesting that the idea to dramatize *The Trumpet Major* was conceived in what is practically Mr. Hardy's native town of Dorchester, the Casterbridge of his novels, within less than three miles of which he was born, where he has resided for the last twenty-five years. The dramatization was done locally by Mr. A. H. Evans, the dramatic coach of the Dorchester Debating and Literary society, under whose auspices the play was produced. All the players live in Dorchester, the scenery was painted from designs of local artists and the uniforms made to measure by a local tailor, some of them being reproductions of the uniforms worn by the Dorset rangers, etc. during the period in question, and most of the music was composed by Mr. Boyton Smith, a well-known Dorchester composer."

The account went on to say that it was a great satisfaction to Hardy that all the talent in the play was local. London talent was offered but he refused it. The wigs were all made locally. The old firelocks and pikes were lent for the occasion by the kindness of Captain Williams of Harrington. The players were using the very fire-locks and pikes used by their ancestors in earnest. In this Hardy no doubt felt that human progress was being made—from the blood-thirsty fact to the appearance of the fact. And the songs sung in the performance, the paper said, were "Budmouth Days," "Valenciennes," "Rollicum-Rorum," and "The Soldier's Tear."

Then from *The Daily Mail* of Thursday, November 27, 1924, I copied the speech of an old farmer to a reporter who had come down to Dorchester from London to write up the local production of *Tess*—speech that sounded as if it came out of one of Hardy's books. "Be ye one o' the folks come to see Tom Hardy's play? There be a lot of such; 'tis in the Corn Hall. Naw, I bean't a-goin' mysen; 'tis proper gloomy, they say, and I can't bear gloom at my age after

a day's work." And from the same paper came the words
of another ancient fellow who talked of the times when he
and Hardy used to swap sums and bread and cheese—
" 'Twas on a bit of greensward by the roadside. He was a
quiet lad, Tom Hardy, a scholar but fonder, I should say,
of a bit of fun in the fields. He became an architect and I
became a printer's boy—six in the morning till nine at night.
And so it was. But I was there at Max Gate when all the
gentlemen from London come to do him honor. He wanted
to put a shawl around my shoulders like he wears himself,
but I said, 'No, Tom, I'm not as old as that yet.' He's a year
older than I am. That was in— These years!"

III

The next day after breakfast I walked the country road
to the old Stinsford Church. While waiting for the service
to begin, I made a sketch of the Hardy graves under their
overspreading cedar tree, the row of the six of them from
north to south with their inscriptions announcing the in-
credibly long lives of the sleepers beneath. The inscription
that interested me most of course was Hardy's: "Here lies
the heart of Thomas Hardy O.M. son of Thomas and
Jemima Hardy. He was born at Upper Bockhampton 2 June
1840 and died at Max Gate Dorchester 11 January 1928.
His ashes rest in poets corner Westminster Abbey."

The vicar, a middle-aged man with a youngish scholar's
face, came by and passed on into the church. The bell began
pealing, and I followed him in for the Sunday morning
service. A few people arrived presently and the service began. I counted the congregation. There were thirty-one
girls and women and three men including myself. The choir
consisted of four—one man with a combination tenor-bass
voice which he soon showed off to loud advantage, and

three girls. The vicar was obviously a learned man, but nervous and halting in his delivery, and for all his earnestness the congregation sat in a sort of sleepy and brooding indifference hardly paying any attention to him or his words, it seemed. And I was reminded of an entry in Hardy's diary which Mrs. Hardy had used in her first volume of the biography of her husband where he speaks of women praying in a church as if under enchantment while their real life is spinning on beneath this apparent one of calm, like the District Railway-trains underground just by—"throbbing, rushing, hot, concerned with next week, last week."

I could hardly listen to the service. The place was full of Hardy influence—of the hundred years of the piety and music-making of his family here, his father, grandfather, uncle, mother, brothers and sisters, and the swarms of characters from his books who had worshipped, fallen from grace, repented, sung, and made music here—the Dewys, the Leafs, the Pennys, the Mails, the Days, and many another.

The minister gave out the hymn, the organist pedalled, and the ragged voice of both choir and congregation rose into the semblance of a song, declaring—

> "Lord, it is my chief complaint
> That my soul is weak and faint;
> Yet I love thee and adore.
> Oh, for grace to love thee more."

He read then from the Book of Micah, adjuring his listeners "to do justly, and to love mercy and to walk humbly with thy God." After this there was a feeble prayer on his part and another bit of scripture reading from St. Luke— "And the Devil said unto him, If thou be the Son of God, command this stone that it be made bread."

Following this, the choir made a pitiful attempt at a chant, in which the tenor-basso's voice roared off in the lead. Just in front of me was a scraggly little woman about fifty or sixty with the thinnest and wrinkledest long neck I ever saw. But she possessed a huge frog-like voice which she poured out with great fervor when she struck a place she could manage. She had a compass of about four notes, and in that range she was terrific, out-doing the tenor-basso even in "Lord, thou hast been our refuge from one generation to another—before the mountains were brought forth, or ever the earth and the world were made."

Again the vicar indulged in a long prayer, and then preached a tiresome sermon on the temptation of Jesus in the wilderness. I was glad when the service was over and I could get out into the fresh air again. I walked back to Dorchester a different way, stopping at Grey's Bridge, where once Fanny Robin rested herself in *Far from the Madding Crowd.* I made a copy of the inscription on a bronze plate embedded in the masonry—

> "Grey's Bridge 1748
> Dorset
> Any person wilfully
> injuring any part of
> this County Bridge
> will be guilty of
> felony and upon
> conviction liable
> to be transported for life."

Back in Dorchester, I called again at Mrs. Major's to return her material on Hardy. I told her I hadn't finished with it all. She asked me to coffee in the evening, saying I could return it then. I went back to the King's Arms and worked on clippings and copying programs and more news items. Then I wrote a note to Mrs. Hardy and took a taxi to Max Gate to deliver it. A middle-aged woman met me at the door, looked at me suspiciously, accepted the note and went away. She came back presently and said Mrs. Hardy would see me. I was shown into the living room of the large but simple red brick house—a room filled with a sort of Victorian feeling—a piano half submerged with bric-a-brac, walls covered with pictures of local scenes, two or three portraits of Hardy, two bookcases partially filled with publishers' copies, etc. Mrs. Hardy came in, a somewhat heavy elderly woman with a pale sweet tired face. She was dressed in simple black, and with cheap black cotton stockings and shoes, and wore a close-fitting, down-hanging brimmed black hat. She asked me to sit. She appeared very ill at ease and kept twisting her hands nervously together as we talked. She gave one a strange impression of utter weariness, helplessness, age and girlishness all combined. Now and then she put her hand to her breast as if worried by some pain or shortness of breath. I regretted that I had come. At last we got on the subject of modern American literature. She liked Willa Cather, thought Sinclair Lewis too caricaturing and somewhat dull except perhaps in *Babbitt* or *Elmer Gantry*.

"Is America like that? It isn't, is it? No."

Finally we got around to Mr. Hardy. As she talked about her husband the same dull tired and sick look remained—her eyes roving about the room continuously. Among other things she said:

—Before he died Mr. Hardy destroyed many and many manuscripts of plots, stories, fragments, etc. And a great many of his first wife's notes and writings too. I tell about that in my book.

—He had a wonderful facility in plot construction. It seemed no effort to him to evolve all sorts of combinations of characters.

—A well-known writer was here once and confessed that he had offered a local story-teller five pounds for every plot he would collect for him. When he had a plot he could write his own story, he said. Like Bach the musician who was so sterile in new motifs,—he was. But not Mr. Hardy.

—Mr. Hardy would write page after page with scarcely any alteration. When the story grew warm or situations exciting and charged with emotion he could write on and on without an error. In the colder passages he had most trouble.

—He wasn't particularly interested in American literature. No. Yes, he had heard of Eugene O'Neill but he had never read anything of his so far as I know.

—The last years of his life he read only poetry—Shakespeare, Keats, Shelley. Shakespeare and Shelley were his favorites. He liked Byron too, very much.

—Yes, the *Greek Anthology* meant a lot to him. Yes, we knew of Mr. Masters' *Spoon River* and liked it. What's become of him? Someone sent me a copy of a later book of his—yes, *Doomsday Book*. It was dull.

—Yes, Schopenhauer was his favorite philosopher and not Hegel, I should say. And Von Hartmann. He read German philosophy a great deal at one time. No doubt its influence showed in *The Dynasts*. Yes.

—I don't see why people continue to hold that Mr. Hardy was so pessimistic. Do you know Mr. Barrie's work? It seems to me he is far more that—one of the most cynical and pessimistic writers I've ever known. He is a friend of ours and came here often before Mr. Hardy died. No, I never heard Mr. Hardy speak about his work. They were very close friends and I suppose they liked what each other wrote. I don't know. Mr. Galsworthy used to come often and Colonel Lawrence, Mr. Masefield and others, many

Americans too. There was a young American woman, a poet here the other day. She lives near the Powyses not far from Dorchester. She's from Charleston. You know her? Ravenel? Pinckney? I don't remember her name.

—Yes, I like Mr. Galsworthy's work, but I don't think he does great work. We both felt there is always something shallow and easy in his people. Perhaps in *The Man of Property* he approached real tragedy. Mr. Hardy liked Masefield's poetry very much. Yes.

—Yes, Mr. Hardy was always interested in the theatre, but he recognized he had little talent for it. Still he liked it, and we used to go up to London to the plays. And he worked closely with the Hardy Players here—helping in any way he could.

—You saw *Tess* produced in London? How did you like it? Yes, I liked Mrs. Bugler as Tess. I didn't like the lady who played Mrs. Sir John up there. Mrs. Major was much better here—much. We both used to feel that Mrs. Bugler had the making of a great tragic actress. But she's rather old to begin now—thirty-three, I think.

—No, I don't think Mr. Hardy ever got the magazine you sent. Who is Mrs. Katherine Gilbert? Yes, I'd like to read what she's written on my husband's work.

—The other day Mr. Galsworthy was down here. He said he thought it would be a hundred years before Mr. Hardy was truly appreciated by the world and had reached his proper place. You don't think so?

—Yes, many people come here, more and more. Many Japanese. There's a great deal of interest in Mr. Hardy's work in Japan. What do you think of him, in America? That's interesting. He's not as popular as Mr. Barrie there, is he? I guess that's true—you either like Hardy or you don't.

—The second part of the *Life* I'm writing will be out I

think in February. I wanted to have it done by this autumn but I was unable to.

—We haven't decided on the type of memorial to my husband yet. Many people want it somewhere in the town. On Egdon Heath? Wouldn't that be too far away? Yes, it would be fitting perhaps, but—I don't know what artist will do it. We have so few good sculptors. Yes, perhaps Epstein might do, but he's rather uncouth and huge. Yes, he might do. We haven't decided yet. Send me the letter Epstein wrote to you. I'll return it.

—His best writing perhaps was at the end of *The Wood-landers*. He liked that, I think, best. Maybe you'd like to look into the garden. When the workmen were excavating for this house they dug up some Roman ware. There's a large piece in the garden. (*She turned and looked out through the window.*) There comes Mr. Hardy's cat, he's been lost. (*She went out and presently returned with a large purring cat of a bluish sooty color.*) We call him Cobby. My husband said when he came to live with us here that we'd have trouble with him. We have. He wanders off and stays for days. When Wessex died, Mr. Hardy's dog, we decided not to have any more pets. But we did adopt Cobby.

—You will excuse me please. I must go to tea across the fields. (*It had been raining and I suggested her riding back in the taxi which had come for me. She seemed embarrassed, but agreed and we set out. The distance was about two miles and I wondered at her idea of walking so far in the wet. We said goodbye.*) Write me if you will, and I shall be glad to help you out with any information you wish. Have you seen Mr. Tilley? He lives down there. There at the Maumsby Rings is where some want the monument.

IV

I went to Mr. Tilley's farther down the road. He was in —a thin-faced high-foreheaded, clever old man. He told me about the Hardy Players and showed me his collection of programs. He, like many other Dorchester people, had a photograph of Hardy on the wall.

—How did the Hardy Players begin? Well we were an old Literary and Debating Society. We'd meet on every Tuesday night and debate all sorts of things—"Resolved that the Duke of Wellington was a greater man than Napoleon" or what not. We had about three hundred members. Once we decided we'd give some plays. We produced *Much Ado*, *Twelfth Night*, and *Taming of the Shrew*. Around 1907 we had a speaker give a lecture on Napoleon. Mr. Evans thought it'd be nice to have something else too. So he got up a scene or two from *The Trumpet Major* dealing with the Napoleonic area—era I should say. It was a big success. So we decided to give other scenes from Hardy. That's how we got started. But we've stopped now. We haven't done anything since we produced *Tess* in 1924. We raised over a thousand pounds for charity.

—Yes, I knew Mr. Hardy well. I dramatized several of the plays, and he would always help me out when I was stuck. I could go to him any time and be welcome. He was a quiet man and very clever at all sorts of things. As you know perhaps he was from a very humble family—real Dorset farmers. Yes, he was always one of us here, and I didn't find him peculiar at all. Of course he had his ways— all great men do. He was a great man. Pictures of the plays? You can get plenty of 'em in London. For every time we had a play the photographers would come down here, and they bothered us a great deal, getting in the way with their cameras and the like. Are you writing a book on Mr. Hardy? No. Well, there's plenty of 'em being written.

From Mr. Tilley's I went out north of the town to see the Poundbury or Pummery Camp, an ancient stronghold covering about twenty acres and where Michael Henchard once held his merrymaking and later stood by its deep silent pool contemplating suicide. From there I saw to the north the famous Wolfeton House which figured in "The Lady Penelope" of *The Group of Noble Dames* and where the lady and her husband were supposed to lie buried. The house dates back to the time of Henry VII and beyond. Farther to the east lay Egdon Heath and Hardy's birthplace.

In the evening I went to Mrs. Major's for after-dinner coffee. She told me much more Hardy lore. And I, now caught in her and Hardy's spell, bought three of her rare programs at a pound each—far too much for my poor pocketbook.

"The Hardy's have almost died out now," she said. "Mr. Hardy never had any children. In fact he seemed to know little about them. He liked pets, animals so much maybe because he never had any little folks of his own. You'll notice in his books that there are never any children except in *Jude*, and they are not very successful as such. Mr. Hardy had one brother and two sisters, none of whom ever married. Mary was his favorite. They seemed to have more in common. The only living one is Kate and she's an old spinster now. There is a cousin in Lower Bockhampton, I think. His brother's name was Henry.

"I guess everybody has told you how quiet and reserved Mr. Hardy was. I remember he used to walk over to Stinsford Church where his wife was buried. He'd go along as if he wanted nobody to notice him. He'd always bring some heath or wild flowers in his hand and put on her grave. When he'd stood there a while he'd likely call by the vicarage. He and the vicar were good friends—Rev. Mr. Cowley, the one you heard preach this morning. He'd ask at the door if any visitors were in. If there were he'd go away, and if not he'd go in and have a cup of tea, walking back later in the evening. He walked everywhere he could, and I've heard him say he missed it a great deal when he couldn't get about well. He didn't like riding in a carriage. And he'd never buy an automobile. Since he died Mrs. Hardy—the present one—has bought one, but she doesn't ride in it much.

"He was quite wealthy when he died. Everybody was surprised at the amount he left. I don't think he himself ever realized how much he was worth. He came from a poor family and was always very saving up to his last days. When he died he was worth about 90,000 pounds.

"I told you how good he was at music and everything. I remember once we had trouble rehearsing the Christmas Mummers in 'The Play of St. George.' This was a little drama he had concocted, as he said, from the memories of his boyhood. It occurs in *The Return of the Native*, as you may remember. He was present when we were rehearsing. Presently he stepped out, tucked his fiddle under his chin and played the old tunes as if he'd known them all his life. And he had, for he was brought up on them by his father and mother. She was a very remarkable woman—his father too for that matter, though, as some said, with more business hindsight than foresight.

"You saw Cobweb? He was a great favorite of Mr. Hardy's and during his last and long illness that cat would stay on his bed for hours.

"As I told you, the second Mrs. Hardy was very devoted to Mr. Hardy. I once heard him say she'd never spent a night from him during their whole married life. She used to go up to London and return the same day, and that's a very hard trip as you no doubt know. Yes, she took care of him well. And he was not easy to take care of. Most great men are not, I suppose.

"He dramatized *Tess* and kept it more than thirty years before it was produced. But I remember I told you that. There was a letter in the paper which he wrote to Henry Arthur Jones, and he says in it that when we wanted to produce it he tried to rewrite it, for the theatre was different from what it was when he first wrote it. But he couldn't get back into the spirit of it, and so he left it as it was. And that's how we played it.

"The worst thing that the Hardy Players ever did was *The Queen of Cornwall*. It was just too difficult. We couldn't do the parts. It was a good play, but we couldn't act in it. Mr. Hardy was nice about it and tried to help us, but it didn't go right."

We said goodbye, and I returned to the King's Arms.